THE
GOD
OF ALL
Comfort

ENCOUNTERING THE GOD WHO HEALS

PRISCILLA SERWAA-BOATENG

Published by BKC Publishing & Consulting
info@bkc.name | +233244961121 | www.BKC.name/consulting

Contact the Author
Email: principlesbooks@gmail.com
Tel: +447498961747

DEDICATION

I dedicate this book to the two-amazing mothers in my life. My biological mother, my mother dearest Janet Osei, thank you for enduring all things to give us a better life, love you Mama J.

To my Auntie and spiritual mother who led me to the Lord and groomed me in prayer and the Word, Kate Nsafoah, your investment in us was not wasted, I love you and appreciate all you did for us.

CONTENTS

ACKNOWLEDGEMENTS

It is said, it takes a village to raise a child, and certainly, it has taken more than a village to raise me. There are many people who have been a part of my journey as a person and as a Christian who are due their honour.

My utmost gratitude goes to my Heavenly Father, my Lord Jesus, and my companion, the Holy Spirit. For the love unending, showing me mercy upon mercy, time after time, time, and again. You have my life and it is yours to use and to keep.

To my family, we have endured the worse together and the bond of love, forgiveness, hope, faith, and perseverance have only grown stronger. I love you Mama and Joe; I know that God is re-writing your stories. Thank you, Mama, for all you have endured making sure we had a place to stay and food to eat. You are a brave and strong woman.

To my siblings, I could not ask for a better bunch to be a part of. You are all amazing! To my big sister Portia, you are a strong force hidden under a calm and gentle spirit, you carried us when we almost fell apart as a family. Your settlement from heaven is due you. To my only brother, Kofi Boateng, you are a blessing and I praise God for the man He has raised you to be. You are a world-changer in the making, and I cannot wait to see your full manifestation. To the heart of my family, Baby Sister Danette, fondly called Danny, you are a breath of fresh air and a joy to our hearts. God knew we needed you and He sent you to remind us of His love. Girl, you are so loved, and I could not imagine life without you.

To the Cole family, thank you for paving the way for us. Looking forward to better days ahead and creating beautiful memories. Mr. &Mrs. Cole, Prince Lillian, Richie, and Mimi, I love you all.

To the two of my best ladies. Mrs. Ivy Nimoh, and Dr. Christina Bediako-Ntumy, my girls. Our times of laugher, joy, tears, and challenges are times we can never forget. We have overcome some difficult times in our lives and with our families. My heart rejoices when I look into all the greatness that is manifesting in our lives now and in our future. Our family vacations will be awesome, you will just have to wait for me to start popping some babies out.

To my Church Family, The Church of Pentecost Canada, you have moulded me into the Woman of Faith I am Today. To all the Apostles, Pastors, and the leadership of the COP Canada, your investments in me are noted in heaven. A special thank you to Apostle Daniel Nii Lomotey Engman for your guidance on this project. Thank you for every prayer, word of encouragement, correction, and direction. The world will know about your work through me, and many others.

Elder and Mrs., Jackson your contributions to my life and that of my family are noteworthy. To my advisor and mother in the Lord, Mama Doris Out-Nyarko, you are a fountain of wisdom and blessings. Thank you for standing with me through the most difficulty time.

To Mr. and Mrs. Nyame (New Era Mart, Toronto) we are grateful for all your love and support.

To my sister Portia and to Dr. Alex Opoku, Ph.D., Associate Professor, University College of London, Thank you for going to the pain of review this book. Alex you have saved me in so many ways and I will forever be grateful.

To Apostle James Mckeown Quainoo, Apostle Alex Gyamena, Pastor Joseph Fynn-Sackey and Pastor Richard Adjei, thank you for your guidance over the years and your devotion to the Youth Ministry of C.O.P Canada.

To Dr. Harriet Ansah, thank you for your support and the time invested in this project. Your forward and your endorsement is well appreciated. Truly you are beyond beautiful.

To everyone who has been part of my journey, who is named and unnamed on this page, I say thank you for being a part of my journey. May the God who blesses, shower you all with His absolute Best.

FOREWORD

The right word at the right time can help us when we need comfort in our suffering, grief, and pain. Comfort! Jesus reminds us in MatThew 5:4 *"Blessed are those who mourn, for they will be comforted"* If we are to keep hearing the voice of God in seasons of pain, despair, grief & suffering we must stay connected to the source; The Holy Spirit who is our comforter.

When we hear the word comfort we usually have thoughts of pain, hurt, disappointments, grief, loss, conflict, and sometimes death. However, the Lord says clearly in Isaiah 41:10 "Don't be afraid for I am with you. Don't be discouraged, for I am your God. I will strengthen you and help you. I will hold you up with my victorious right hand" Our inner man will not be unsettled if we know that God is The God Of All Comfort

Hurt and pain are guaranteed in this world. Scripture tells us that we will have trouble and tribulation while here on earth but He instructs us that we can take heart because He has overcome the world! (John 16:33)

Priscilla Serwaa-Boateng has written a book that answers questions about grief, comfort, suffering, the cross, compensation and restoration from a biblical and personal stand point. The God Of All Comfort creates an understanding that equips and prepares us for uncertain sudden seasons. We must know the foundation of grief and suffering, we must know and understand the price of the cross and what it cost Jesus, we must accept the compassionate and restoration of the father if we must move on to our next level.

In The God Of All Comfort Priscilla Serwaa-Boateng leads us into the most in-depth understanding of WHY and HOW to embrace God as your comforter because by accepting His comfort, the cycle of grief and pain is broken.

As believers, we know that God is faithful, and is always looking over us to comfort us. He truly cares and is our protector and comforter in times of need. In the heat of despair, we must remind ourselves of these truths about God and His son Jesus who paid the price for our ultimate freedom and victory. We may get knocked down but we will never get knocked out because The God Of All Comfort is ever-present.

With everything going on in the world, we must never forget He is The God Of All Comfort. He is always in command and will restore. This is an awesome time for believers to embrace His love and comfort and extend such grace to others.

Whatever the circumstance may be, we can use comforting verses from the Bible and use this on-time book to find a peace that surpasses understanding.

We thank you, Priscilla Serwaa-Boateng for a book to assist us all in the times ahead. Thank God for The God Of All Comfort. Our healing is secured in Him.

REV DR. HARRIET ANSAH
*(Co-pastor at Faith International Church,
Founder of Beyond My Beauty Ministries - Canada)*

INTRODUCTION

Grief, sorrow, sadness are emotions we experience as part of our humanity. These we have experienced and will experience in certain seasons of our lives. While sadness and sorrow may be a part of our human journey, there must come a time when we experience joy and happiness. Grief must not be a perpetual and enduring part of our lives.

Weeping may endure for a night, But [c]joy comes in the morning. (Psalm 30:5b)

Grief can be defined as an intense sorrow caused by a loss or disappointment. It can also be caused by many things such as losing a loved one, a divorce, losing a job, a failure in business, or challenges in ministry. Grief can be caused by our own mistakes, other people's mistakes, an attack from the enemy, and sometimes life in general can cause us grief.

The consolation we have is that we have a God who does not discriminate on who to heal or what to heal. The Apostle

Paul calls Him the God of all comfort.

Blessed be the God and Father of our Lord Jesus Christ, the Father of mercies and God of all comfort, who comforts us in all our tribulation, that we may be able to comfort those who are in any [a]trouble, with the comfort with which we ourselves are comforted by God. For as the sufferings of Christ abound in us, so our [b]consolation also abounds through Christ.

2 Corinthians 1:3

I have personally experienced grief coming from a broken home and having many personal failures including going through a rough divorce. If anyone knows what it means to grieve, I know that very well. In the same token, I am also the one who has experienced the Love of God and the comfort of the Holy Spirit in its extremity. It is then on this basis that I write this book to share with you the joy of receiving the comfort of God even in the deepest of sorrows.

We will explore the various stories of grief in the Bible along with my personal journey and see how God through the comfort of the Holy Spirit, brought healing in all these situations.

It is my prayer that as you turn the pages of this book, you will not only identify with my sorrow but that you will also meet the God who is able to heal and make you whole.

CHAPTER ONE

THE FOUNDATION OF GRIEF & SUFFERING

The question has always been asked, 'If God is a good God, why is there so much suffering in the world? As we are dealing with the subject of Grief and Comfort, it is imperative to dig into the foundation of all human suffering. There may be many reasons why people experience grief and in our own individual lives, we may experience different seasons of grief as a result of different causes. Yet the foundation of all human suffering remains the same; sin, and the fall of man.

The Bible is full of stories of people who experienced tremendous grief yet overcame and had a change of story through the help of God. That tells me that no matter the magnitude of your pain, there is hope for you. For those of us who are Christians, who believe in the Lord Jesus, who are called believers, the hope we have is that God can and makes all things new. If you are reading this book and you are not a Christian, may I humbly invite you to welcome the Lord Jesus Christ into your heart? I can say without a shadow of a doubt that He is able to heal, renew, and restore your life and bring wholeness and joy as you have never experienced. He is the reason I can talk about my grief, and my healing with such joy because He has done such a great work of healing my heart that, it feels like it was never broken. Oh, how He loves the world!

For God so loved the world that He gave His only begotten Son, that whoever believes in Him should not perish but have everlasting life. For God did not send His Son into the world to condemn the world, but that the world through Him might be saved.

John 3:16-17

THE FALL OF MAN

The story of the Fall of Man in Genesis 3 gives a rendering of how man lost his position with God through the cunning deception of the enemy. Deception is Satan's greatest weapon, the very first weapon he deployed against man and still the foundational arsenal upon which he launches all his assaults. The disobedience of man made him lose his place of safety and security with God.

We can trace every hurt, disappointment, and wound back to sin, disobedience, the weakness, and or the wickedness of man inspired by the enemy. Often, we have a situation that turns out to be extremely painful to our surprise, and that is because the enemy has been playing the same trick with us as he did with the first man and the first woman. The fact of the matter is, we have an enemy who is enraged with us and in every situation, orchestrates situations and manipulates people to hurt others or even ourselves.

To understand the depth of the hatred of the enemy, let us consider the following text.

Revelations 12

Now a great sign appeared in heaven: a woman clothed with the sun, with the moon under her feet, and on her head a garland of twelve stars. Then being with child, she cried out in labor and in pain to give birth.

And another sign appeared in heaven: behold, a great, fiery red dragon having seven heads and ten horns, and seven diadems on his heads. His tail drew a third of the stars of heaven and threw them to the earth. And the dragon stood before the woman who was ready to give birth, to devour her Child as soon as it was born. She bore a male Child who was to rule all nations with a rod of iron. And her Child was caught up to God and His throne. Then the woman fled into the wilderness, where she has a place prepared by God, that they should feed her there one thousand two hundred and sixty days.

Satan Thrown Out of Heaven

And war broke out in heaven: Michael and his angels fought with the dragon; and the dragon and his angels fought, 8 but they [a]did not prevail, nor was a place found for [b]them in heaven any longer. So the great dragon was cast out, that serpent of old, called the Devil and Satan, who deceives the whole world; he was cast to the earth, and his angels were cast out with him.

Then I heard a loud voice saying in heaven, "Now salvation, and strength, and the kingdom of our God, and the power of

His Christ have come, for the accuser of our brethren, who accused them before our God day and night, has been cast down. And they overcame him by the blood of the Lamb and by the word of their testimony, and they did not love their lives to the death. *Therefore rejoice, O heavens, and you who dwell in them! Woe to the inhabitants of the earth and the sea! For the devil has come down to you, having great wrath, because he knows that he has a short time."*

The Woman Persecuted

Now when the dragon saw that he had been cast to the earth, he persecuted the woman who gave birth to the male Child. But the woman was given two wings of a great eagle, that she might fly into the wilderness to her place, where she is nourished for a time and times and half a time, from the presence of the serpent. So the serpent spewed water out of his mouth like a flood after the woman, that he might cause her to be carried away by the flood. 16 But the earth helped the woman, and the earth opened its mouth and swallowed up the flood which the dragon had spewed out of his mouth. And the dragon was enraged with the woman, and he went to make war with the rest of her offspring, who keep the commandments of God and have the testimony of Jesus [c]Christ.

Revelations 12:1-17

There are four things that I would like us to note from this text. Now there have been many interpretations of this portion of scripture and the primary interpretation of this text is the representation of Christ and His Church. However, for the purposes of this book, we look at how this scripture applies to our lives individually and also as a cooperate body,

4

being part of God's creation and His agenda for the world.

THE CHARACTERS IN THIS STORY
- The woman-You
- The serpent-Satan
- God
- Angels of God

The woman was pregnant with a child. Every person is born with a desire, a vision, and a dream to do something and become the person that God intended them to be. Our dreams and aspirations may vary but every God-given vision is valid. Our God-given dreams and visions all work as part of God's agenda for humanity.

It is imperative for you to understand that you are part of God's plans. He is counting on the gifts, talents, wisdom and all the goodness He hid in you to manifest for the benefit of society. You are important and your dreams are valid.

For we are his workmanship, created in Christ Jesus for good works, which God prepared beforehand, that we should walk in them.

Ephesians 2:10

God created us for His pleasure in His image that we should be the continuity of His creative power. The fact is that God has prepared for each of us the works that we must walk in to fulfil His purposes. We are an extension of Himself, He fulfils his purposes on Earth through us therefore the enemy being at odds with God, fights everything and everyone who bears the image of God, even unbelievers.

A scientist who may be an unbeliever may be stirred to find the cure for a disease. In the year 2020 as I am writing this book, the world is plagued by the Covid-19 pandemic, also known as the Corona Virus. This is a deadly virus that has infected thousands of people across all continents of the world. There is not a place in this world that has not been affected by this virus. As of yet, there is no cure for this virus. Now a scientist or a group of scientists may be stirred to find the cure for this virus and to them, the means of finding the cure is through research. We know however that everything that there is to be discovered has already been created by God. It can be discovered because it was created.

In our lives, we can experience a tsunami of evil, like the enemy spurring evil from his mouth to take away everything that we hold so dearly. He attacks our marriages, children, relationship, our careers, businesses, and our health. The worse is that sometimes we can experience all these things at the same time, thus one thing after the other. Hence, the phrase, "when it rains, it pours".
While the above may bring us to a place of helplessness, we must remember that we are not without help for there is always help in God for us. The Bible is filled with many stories of Hope.

"For there is hope for a tree, if it is cut down, that it will sprout again, and that its tender shoots will not cease. Though its root may grow old in the earth, and its stump may die in the ground, yet at the scent of water it will bud and bring forth

branches like a plant."

Job 14:7-9.

As you are reading this book, you may be going through a painful season, the death of a loved one, a divorce, loss of an opportunity, or a job loss, or suffering as a result of your mistakes or other people's mistakes. Let me assure you, there is hope for you; a brighter day will come. When I was going through my divorce at the age of 32, I could see no way out of the heart-wrenching pain. I felt like my world had ended. There were times I would wake up and go right back to bed because I could not bring myself to face the day. I felt so broken and so helpless. But there is hope, and that hope is Jesus, who makes all things beautiful again.

WHERE IS GOD IN MY PAIN?
You may be asking where is God in my pain? Well, I know what the enemy does is to cause me pain but what is God saying about my grief, or what is God saying about grief in general?

Well, let us see what the Bible has to say. Let us take a look at the book of Luke.

So He came to Nazareth, where He had been brought up. And as His custom was, He went into the synagogue on the Sabbath day, and stood up to read. 17 And He was handed the book of the prophet Isaiah. And when He had opened the book, He found the place where it was written:
"The Spirit of the Lord is upon Me,
Because He has anointed Me

To preach the gospel to the poor;
He has sent Me [i]to heal the brokenhearted,
To proclaim liberty to the captives
And recovery of sight to the blind,
To set at liberty those who are [j]oppressed;
To proclaim the acceptable year of the Lord."

Luke 4:17-19

We see in this scripture that Jesus had just come out from a 40 day fast and many described this passage as the ministry statement of Jesus Christ. Jesus declares the purpose of His ministry in that statement. That is, He came to preach the Gospel, heal the broken-hearted, set the captives free, restore insight, and perspective aright. This is to say, it is the will of the Lord to heal every grief and for every pain, there is an anointing to comfort.

'Where is God in my pain?' is a question that many people are asking and, in my opinion, it is a valid question that God seeks to answer. I have asked this question many times but the challenge with many people is that they ask this question yet are not willing to receive the answer or are not willing to do what the answer demands in other to receive help from God.

When I asked this question during my painful divorce, I had to brace myself for the answer that came, and I had to accept the answer although it was not pleasant. Many of us like to accuse God of things without taking personal responsibility or be accountable for our wrongdoings and our disobedience. You may be thinking, where are you going with this, I thought this was a book about receiving the

8

comfort of God? Yes, it is, but wholeness comes from truth and the pain of remaining stagnant in your pain or situation is worse than the pain of facing the truth of God about your situation and receiving His healing.

And you shall know the truth, and the truth shall make you free.

John 8:32

The enemy wants you to operate in grey shadows, and never come to the place of knowing the truth behind your pain, that is his weapon and power over you. But God wants us to know the truth behind our suffering and in so doing, we are empowered to seek permanent solutions instead of temporary comfort. Do not let the enemy comfort you with deception and keep you in bondage.

For me that moment of truth came when I was angrily yelling at God and calling out my "Christian Girl' accolades; that I had been serving God all my life, I kept myself, I went into covenant with you…and on and on. And the Lord gave me an answer that shook my being. He reminded me of things He told me before and during the marriage that I did not completely adhere to that could have kept me from going through the pain of a divorce. Oh, that shut me up alright. I immediately changed my tone from 'Lord why did you do this to me?!' to 'Lord what do we do now?'. This was the turning point that began my healing. We often neglect the voice of God and lead ourselves into tremendous pain and trouble. And yes, I was disgracefully mistreated, abused, and reproached and went through great difficulties due to the weakness and wickedness of men. Yet before that and in the midst of that, God gave me a prompting to help me escape that pain, yet I did not fully adhere to his voice.

Now, prior to the marriage, there were signs, dreams, dreams from other people that was a caution from the Lord. The Lord wanted to spare me from the pain the shame that was ahead of me, but I did not let Him. I refused through my disobedience. We will return to details of this matter in later chapters.

In the next chapter, we are going to look at people in the bible who went through tremendous pain, grief, and loss yet came through situations that seemed impossible to recover from because they hoped in God and held on to His word. They overcame and their lives were turned around as if they had not even experienced that kind of pain.

CHAPTER TWO

BIBLICAL STORIES OF GRIEF AND COMFORT
JACOB: THE STORY OF LOSS LOVE, EMPLOYMENT INEQUITY, DEATH, AND RESTORATION

The life of Jacob is one story filled with painful experiences of disappointment, loss, inequality, and even death. His story begins as one of the twin sons of Isaac, on whom the blessing was given. Even before their birth, these twin brothers, Esau and Jacob were struggling for dominance even in the womb.

Now many questions the means through which Jacob obtained the blessing from his father, yet according to the agenda of God, Jacob was to be the carrier of the blessing promised to Abraham. Jacob as a means to obtain his father's blessing outwitted his father into believing that he was his brother Esau *(this story is found in Genesis 27)*. To save his life from the sword of his brother Esau, Jacob left his father's house to stay with his Uncle Laban in Haran (Genesis 27: 41-45)

As he entered the city of Haran, Jacob encountered a woman whom he fell in love with and would labour 14 years to have her in marriage. Rachel, the daughter of Laban, Jacob's uncle was the desire of Jacobs's heart and after serving his uncle for 7 years in exchange for receiving Rachel as a wife, Leah was given Jacob to fulfil the custom that the older daughter must marry before the younger sister does. Jacob was painfully cheated by his uncle Laban and had to work another 7 years for the woman he genuinely loved. Although Jacob had laboured most of his adult life for Laban, Laban was still not satisfied and sought to send Jacob away empty-handed without what we would call, a severance package in our current employment terms. The passage below explains Jacob's conversation with His wives concerning their father's treatment of him.

Now Jacob heard the words of Laban's sons, saying, "Jacob has taken away all that was our father's, and from what was our father's he has acquired all this wealth." And Jacob saw the countenance of Laban, and indeed it was not favourable toward him as before. Then the Lord said to Jacob, "Return to the land of your fathers and to your family, and I will be with you."

So Jacob sent and called Rachel and Leah to the field, to his flock, and said to them, "I see your father's [a]countenance, that it is not favourable toward me as before; but the God of my father has been with me. And you know that with all my might I have served your father. Yet your father has deceived me and changed my wages ten times, but God did not allow him to hurt me. If he said thus: 'The speckled shall be your wages,' then all the flocks bore speckled. And if he said thus: 'The streaked shall be your wages,' then all the flocks bore streaked. So God has taken away the livestock of your father and given them to me.

"And it happened, at the time when the flocks conceived, that I lifted my eyes and saw in a dream, and behold, the rams which leaped upon the flocks were streaked, speckled, and grey-spotted. Then the Angel of God spoke to me in a dream, saying, 'Jacob.' And I said, 'Here I am.' And He said, 'Lift your eyes now and see, all the rams which leap on the flocks are streaked, speckled, and grey-spotted; for I have seen all that Laban is doing to you. I am the God of Bethel, where you anointed the pillar and where you made a vow to Me. Now arise, get out of this land, and return to the land of your family.'

Genesis 31:1-10

The story above depicts a situation between an employer and an employee and in this situation, Jacob being the employee and Laban being the employer. Jacob had served and dedicated his life to Laban and his children, yet he was constantly taken advantage of. However, amid it all God was with him and in Jacob's own words, "God did not allow Laban to hurt him".

You may have been disappointed or hurt, or unjustly dismissed from your place of work or your business partners may have taken advantage of you. Such situations can cause one to be bitter, angry, and discouraged, feeling that you have laboured in vain. But trust that God sees when you are wronged and when you are taken advantage of and He can make things right if you let him.

LESSONS FROM JACOB IN LABAN'S HOUSE

1. Jacob knew the God of his father. He knew God and could recognize the voice of God when God spoke.

2. He was the carrier of a blessing, yet he went through great difficulty. That is, we may have the promises of God spoken over our lives yet can go through seasons of great difficulty. These difficulties create opportunities for God to move on our behalf.

3. Jacob served diligently. He knew he was being cheated yet he continued to serve his master. Believers are called to be diligent even when it looks like we are being taken advantage of.

4. For a time, it seemed that God was silent and did not rebuke Laban or say anything about Jacob's suffering. Sometimes, God may seem silent in our pain, yet he is not unaware of our challenges

5. Jacob knew how to receive instructions from God and move when God says move. We sometimes find ourselves in situations where we end up getting hurt and taken advantage of because we missed the voice and the direction of God when he asked us to take a step that would protect us from impending danger. There is wisdom in hearing the voice of God and obeying it.

It is the will of God to protect us from harm. Yet He requires our obedience even when we do not understand what He is up to. You may find yourself in a situation, place, or relationship where everything seems to be going on perfectly well at that time and the Lord may speak to you about what is to come. Such warnings may come through dreams, scriptures that the Lord may whisper to you, prophetic words, your discernment (what others call intuition). Do not ignore it. There are stories of people who escaped death, tragedies, and bad relationships because they heeded to the voice of God. On the contrary, others had suffered great losses because they disobeyed the voice of God. It is costly to live in disobedience. The direction of God may require you to leave behind something or someone that looks and seems really "good" and in the natural, it may be difficult to do so as it may seem like a "loss", but you have to trust that if God will ask you to leave something behind, it is because He has something better in mind and wants to protect you from harm.

Remember the former things of old: for I am God, and there is none else; I am God, and there is none like me, 10 Declaring the end from the beginning, and from ancient times the things that are not yet done, saying, My counsel shall stand, and I will do all my pleasure.

Isaiah 46:9-10

GOD'S HEART FOR THE OUTCAST

Often when we read the Bible we see people whose lives we may think that we cannot align with or we cannot identify with because they seemed like good people and we may feel our lives are a mess and as a matter of fact we may be in some troubles that truth be told, we brought on ourselves. This leads us to think that God cannot and will not do for us what He did in the Bible times. But I can assure you that the same God who comforted the people of old is still interested in bringing healing to you. The requirement is to repent and believe.

AN OUTCAST WOUNDED BY GOD'S PEOPLE

Hagar was a maid in Abraham's household, catering to the needs of Lady Sarah. She was not part of the conversation between God, Abraham, and Sarah. She was a simple maidservant, minding her own business until Sarah had a "brilliant" idea to solicit her help in fulfilling the promise of God.

Thus, Sarah gave Hagar to Abraham her husband so they can conceive and have a child for her. Yet this was not part of God's plan for the couple. We need to understand that if we are going to do business with God, we cannot take shortcuts. And this has been my personal experience. Anytime I have moved ahead of God or not trusted in His divine timing and taken the initiative to do things on my own, I either end up getting hurt, disappointed, wasting time, or hurting someone in the process.

The pain of disobedience is not worth the temporary solution you seek, do not do it. Let us consider Hagar and Ishmael's story in the text below:

So, the child grew and was weaned. And Abraham made a great feast on the same day that Isaac was weaned.

And Sarah saw the son of Hagar the Egyptian, whom she had borne to Abraham, scoffing.[c] Therefore she said to Abraham, "Cast out this bondwoman and her son; for the son of this bondwoman shall not be heir with my son, namely with Isaac." And the matter was very [d]displeasing in Abraham's sight because of his son.

But God said to Abraham, "Do not let it be displeasing in your sight because of the lad or because of your bondwoman. Whatever Sarah has said to you, listen to her voice; for in Isaac your seed shall be called. Yet I will also make a nation of the son of the bondwoman, because he is your [e]seed."

So Abraham rose early in the morning, and took bread and [f]a skin of water; and putting it on her shoulder, he gave it and the boy to Hagar, and sent her away. Then she departed and wandered in the Wilderness of Beersheba. And the water in the skin was used up, and she placed the boy under one of the shrubs. Then she went and sat down across from him at about a bowshot; for she said to herself, "Let me not see the death of the boy." So she sat opposite him, and lifted her voice and wept.

And God heard the voice of the lad. Then the angel of God called to Hagar out of heaven, and said to her, "What ails you, Hagar? Fear not, for God has heard the voice of the lad where he is. Arise, lift up the lad and hold him with your hand, for I will make him a great nation."

Then God opened her eyes, and she saw a well of water. And she went and filled the skin with water and gave the lad a drink. So God was with the lad; and he grew and dwelt in the wilderness and became an archer. 21 He dwelt in the Wilderness of Paran; and his mother took a wife for him from the land of Egypt.

Genesis 21:8-21

In the text above, we see Hagar and her son being cast out of

17

his father's house due to the rivalry between the two women, Sarah and Hagar. The very "solution" Sarah created turned out to be a problem in her household. Now, on the part of Hagar, while many usually diminish her pain and blame her for insubordination, we must not also forget that she and her son were victims of Sarah's impatience.

You may have gone through seasons where you were hurt by God's people and this can be one of the most painful situations. It is one thing to be hurt by unbelievers but to be hurt in the church or by Godly people who God has favoured and will continue to favour, can be difficult to comprehend and to go through.

Like Hagar, I went through a difficult season where I was deeply wounded by God's people. I went through a deep emotional abuse and had many things said about me that were simply not true and the worst part of it is that these accusations came from people of faith who has a credible track record of serving the Lord and being faithful, therefore their false testimony about me were believed by many; and I felt broken and deeply wounded. There was no way to defend myself because they were people in authority and had great influence and I was no match and was totally helpless in defending myself. Ha how was I to defend myself and who would believe me?

Like Hagar, I pressed on to God in prayers and in tears and the Lord gave me His word, that if I will let go of this situation and trust it into His hands, He will be the one to vindicate me. Another time in prayer while crying out to

God, I heard Him clearly say, "I was there, I saw everything that happened, and I will settle this matter", and that settled my heart, then he led me to Psalm 10:14

But you, God, see the trouble of the AFflicted; you consider their grief AND TAKE it in HAND. The victims commit themselves to you; you ARe the helper of the FATHERLESS.

This scripture came to me as a direct rhema, just as He saw the tears of Hagar in the wilderness and made provisions for her and the child Ishmael. He introduced Himself as El Roi, the God who sees. He saw my tears, consoled, and assured me of His vindication. Now God's vindication does not mean He is going to hurt others to satisfy you. He is a God who can vindicate you and compensate you without hurting others and we will look into that in later chapters. In God's agenda, there is always room for the outcast. There is always room for healing and reconciliation for the outcast. The grace of God is so great that even when His own people hurt others, He is able to still honour and cover His people and also cover the victim.

In the moment of hurt, you might be tempted to be bitter, disrespectful, and rebellious and think, how could "the so-called" people of God do this to me, but it is always imperative to remember that they are human being with flaws and are also prone to make mistakes and especially when they feel the need to cover their own, they humanity would show more than you would expect, yet in the midst of this God is able to heal and compensate all grievances and losses. It is also important to keep in mind that when the enemy is on a tangent to hurt, and to destroy, his attacks can come through anybody, even God's people. Only be sure that you do not let the wrong done to you cause to you do wrong because of anger and bitterness.

LESSONS FROM HAGAR STORY

1. It matters what we do while we wait on the promises of God. Sarah rushed ahead of God and created a problem that is beyond human capacity to correct, even to this day.
2. Whenever we step out of the will of God, we risk hurting ourselves and those close to us.
3. Sometimes, we can be victims of other people's decisions and mistakes, yet God has a way of compensating us
4. Being hurt or rejected by God's people does not mean God has rejected us.
5. Genuine, well-meaning, God's people can make mistakes, yet God still forgives and honours them.
6. If you are a victim of the mistakes of God's people, turn your heart to God and let Him be the one to heal and make up for every wrongdoing you have suffered.

WOUNDED BY YOUR OWN BLOOD
The Story of Joseph

I remember as a child, anytime time I would go out to play and get myself into some kind of trouble, I would quickly run home to the safety and protection of my loved ones and this is the default reaction of every child. We run home for safety and comfort. The home is supposed to be a place of safety, comfort, and a haven of protection. Yet for many people, their deepest wounds have come from their families. Many young people are on the streets due to the pain and toxicity they experience at home.

This kind of pain is one that can be very damaging. Thankfully, I have been blessed with a lovely and supportive family and we stick together to support each other in the most difficult times. But for many people, this institution that is supposed to bring them security is the very one that ushers them into a world of pain. You find in many homes' children living with abusive parents, damaging sibling rivalry, and sometimes elder abuse. While sibling rivalry is considered a norm or even considered a healthy competition, it can be the source of damaging emotions and rejection for many people.

I know a person who has not lived to his fullest potential due to the rivalry between him and his brother that started at a young age. Even In their adulthood as men, one brother takes the chance every time he gets to undermine the other and have managed to win the love and respect of his parents at the expense of the other brother. It is important that as members of the same household, we do good to each other and not hurt one another.

As we have therefore opportunity, let us do good unto all men, especially unto them who are of the household of faith.
Galatians 6:10

If you have suffered loss and pain from close relatives, God has a place of healing for you as well. Let's take at a look at Joseph's journey with his brothers, Genesis 37.

Now Jacob dwelt in the land where his father was a[a] stranger, in the land of Canaan. This is the history of Jacob. Joseph, being seventeen years old, was feeding the flock with his brothers. And the lad was with the sons of Bilhah and the sons of Zilpah, his father's wives; and Joseph brought a bad report of them to his father. Now Israel loved Joseph more than all his children, because he was the son of his old age. Also he made him a tunic of many colors. But when his brothers saw that their father loved him more than all his brothers, they hated him and could not speak peaceably to him.

Now Joseph had a dream, and he told it to his brothers; and they hated him even more. So he said to them, "Please hear this dream which I have dreamed: There we were, binding sheaves in the field. Then behold, my sheaf arose and also stood upright; and indeed your sheaves stood all around and bowed down to my sheaf."

And his brothers said to him, "Shall you indeed reign over us? Or shall you indeed have dominion over us?" So they hated him even more for his dreams and for his words.

Then he dreamed still another dream and told it to his brothers, and said, "Look, I have dreamed another dream. And this time, the sun, the moon, and the eleven stars bowed down to me." So he told it to his father and his brothers; and his father rebuked him and said to him, "What is this dream that you have dreamed? Shall your mother and I and your brothers indeed come to bow down to the earth before you?" 11 And his brothers envied him, but his father kept the matter in mind.

Joseph Sold by His Brothers

Then his brothers went to feed their father's flock in Shechem. And Israel said to Joseph, "Are not your brothers feeding the flock in Shechem? Come, I will send you to them."
So he said to him, "Here I am."

Then he said to him, "Please go and see if it is well with your brothers and well with the flocks, and bring back word to me." So he sent him out of the Valley of Hebron, and he went to Shechem.

Now a certain man found him, and there he was, wandering in the field. And the man asked him, saying, "What are you seeking?"
So he said, "I am seeking my brothers. Please tell me where they are feeding their flocks."

And the man said, "They have departed from here, for I heard them say, 'Let us go to Dothan.' " So Joseph went after his brothers and found them in Dothan.

Now when they saw him afar off, even before he came near them, they conspired against him to kill him. 19 Then they said to one another, "Look, this [b]dreamer is coming! 20 Come therefore, let us now kill him and cast him into some pit; and we shall say, 'Some wild beast has devoured him.' We shall see what will become of his dreams!"

But Reuben heard it, and he delivered him out of their hands, and said, "Let us not kill him." And Reuben said to them, "Shed no blood, but cast him into this pit which is in the wilderness, and do not lay a hand on him"—that he might deliver him out of their hands, and bring him back to his father.

So it came to pass, when Joseph had come to his brothers, that they stripped Joseph of his tunic, the tunic of many colors that was on him. Then they took him and cast him into a pit. And the pit was empty; there was no water in it.

And they sat down to eat a meal. Then they lifted their eyes and looked, and there was a company of Ishmaelites, coming from Gilead with their camels, bearing spices, balm, and myrrh, on their way to carry them down to Egypt. So Judah said to his brothers, "What profit is there if we kill our brother and conceal his blood? Come and let us sell him to the Ishmaelites, and let not our hand be upon him, for he is our brother and our flesh." And his brothers listened. Then Midianite traders passed by; so the brothers pulled Joseph up and lifted him out of the pit, and sold him to the Ishmaelites for twenty shekels of silver. And they took Joseph to Egypt.

Then Reuben returned to the pit, and indeed Joseph was not in the pit; and he tore his clothes. 30 And he returned to his brothers and said, "The lad is no more; and I, where shall I go?"

So they took Joseph's tunic, killed a kid of the goats, and dipped the tunic in the blood. Then they sent the tunic of many colours, and they brought it to their father and said, "We have found this. Do you know whether it is your son's tunic or not?" And he recognized it and said, "It is my son's tunic. A wild beast has devoured him. Without doubt Joseph is torn to
24

pieces." Then Jacob tore his clothes, put sackcloth on his waist, and mourned for his son many days. And all his sons and all his daughters arose to comfort him; but he refused to be comforted, and he said, "For I shall go down into the grave to my son in mourning." Thus his father wept for him.

Now the [c]Midianites had sold him in Egypt to Potiphar, an officer of Pharaoh and captain of the guard.

Genesis 37:1-36

The story of Joseph as painful and sorrowful as it is, begs the question, can the will of God lead me into danger? There are many lessons to be learned in this chapter and besides the obvious lessons of misunderstanding, there are deeper questions to be asked, can the will of God be fulfilled while causing me pain?

The dynamics of Joseph's relationship with his brothers was one that required his brothers to exercise patience and understanding. The Bible records that Joseph was born to Jacob at a time when Jacob was well into his old age. Thus, the older siblings were much older than Joseph. Scholars believe that the age gap between Reuben and Joseph would be about 12-15 years, thus, before Benjamin was born, Joseph was the baby in the family. Naturally, most parents are drawn to their youngest child especially if they were born to them at a later part of their lives. Having a sister who is 18years younger than I am, we find that as a family that we take delight in her as she is the baby of the family. It's very obvious that our mother treats her with much greater affection than the rest of us but it has never and will never be a root of contention, as a

25

matter of fact, we all treat her better than we treat the rest of
our siblings and that is because there is that understanding
that she is the baby of the family. She gets all the love, gifts
and also runs errands for all her 4 parents. Thus, instead of
Joseph's siblings taking offense at their father's affection for
his young son, they could have taken that as an opportunity
to love on their youngest brother. In our lives and in our
families, we are constantly presented with situations that we
can view as an opportunity to lavish love on others or take
offense on the innocent.

On the other hand, we can see the hand of God in the midst
of the wickedness of Joseph's brothers. Reuben, being the
oldest thought in his heart to save his younger brother by
keeping him in the valley and rescuing him later. This was an
opportunity for God to also rescue Joseph, yet it pleased the
Lord that Joseph should be sold into slavery. Like Joseph,
the Lord Jesus was also placed in danger and suffered many
hardships and grief in order to fulfil the purposes of God.

*Yet it pleased the Lord to [q]bruise Him; He has put Him to
grief. When You make His soul an offering for sin, He shall see
His seed, He shall prolong His days, And the pleasure of the
Lord shall prosper in His hand.*

Isaiah 53:10

Note that the will of God can also lead us into danger and cause
us grief. You may have gone through a difficult time or the
Lord may have called you into a particular situation, maybe
into a job, church, ministry, project, or even relationship and
it seems that you are constantly facing challenges that are

causing you pain and grief and you are wondering, 'is this from the Lord?' I do not know your specific situation and can't say whether it is the will of God for you or not. But it is always wise and essential, especially in these current seasons of uncertainty to hear the voice of God in every situation. Seek Him and find out His will concerning every situation. You need to ask, 'is this from you, or is this an attack of the enemy or the workings of the flesh?'.

Believers in this generation must come to terms with the fact that suffering is part of our Christian journey. The Christian faith that we hold on to at this time has been tried and tested and proven over the years. The fathers of faith fought and endured to preserve the genuineness and sanctity of the gospel to be handed down to us. While we seek healing and consolation for the pain and sufferings we encounter on our journey, we must remember there is a cross laid up for every believer to take on for the sake of our faith. There is no glory without a cross.

But what things were gain to me, these I have counted loss for Christ. Yet indeed I also count all things loss for the excellence of the knowledge of Christ Jesus my Lord, for whom I have suffered the loss of all things, and count them as rubbish, that I may gain Christ and be found in Him, not having my own righteousness, which is from the law, but that which is through faith in Christ, the righteousness which is from God by faith; that I may know Him and the power of His resurrection, and the fellowship of His sufferings, being conformed to His death.
Philippians 3:8-10

Persecution is part of the journey. I believe we are entering an era where we will begin to see the persecutions spoken of concerning the end times. It's not going to be church as usual; we must be willing fight and take up our cross in these end times.

Wherefore gird up the loins of your mind, be sober, and hope to the end for the grace that is to be brought unto you at the revelation of Jesus Christ.

1 Peter 1:13

The life and sufferings of Joseph was a prototype of what the believer's life is like as he journeys and fights to fulfil the purposes of God for his life. The jealousy of Joseph's brothers caused them to sell him into slavery. While they had an evil intent to send him away to avoid seeing him get the love and attention of their father, little did they know they were cooperating with the will and purposes of God. Yes, after going through immense suffering in Egypt, Joseph rose to power and the purposes of God was fulfilled in his life.

We face difficulty in our pursuit of purpose because God takes us through these challenges to prepare us for the life He has for us. We face difficulty also as part of satanic resistance to the manifestation of our purpose. Satan puts up resistance to keep us from reaching our place of destiny, our destiny works together to fulfil God's agenda. I always have this pictorial image in my mind of God calling each one of us in His presence and saying, "I have these plans for you because I want to partner with you to accomplish my purposes but in order to achieve that, these are the challenges you must overcome", listing every difficulty and resistance that will come our way.

Without the healthy view of suffering as part of the Christian journey, we will seek and demand comfort and forfeit the very best of God for our lives because we loved comfort much more than paying the price to achieve destiny.

LESSON FROM JOSEPH AND HIS BROTHERS

1. The stability and sanctity of a family depends on understanding. *Through wisdom a house is built, and by understanding it is established; By knowledge, the rooms are filled. With all precious and pleasant riches."* (*Proverbs 24:3-4*)
2. The will of God can lead you to deep dark places.
3. Your suffering may be sanctioned by God to fulfil His intended purposes.
4. Do not always be looking to man for help. God will sometimes block and stop people from getting you out of that trouble until His purposes are accomplished.
5. God can make you flourish even in adversity and in the place of your affliction. You just need to persevere through it.
6. And the name of the second he called Ephraim: *"For God has caused me to be fruitful in the land of my affliction."* (*Genesis 41:52*)
7. If your suffering was sanctioned by God, you cannot be upset with the people and instruments He used. *"But as for you, you meant evil against me; but God meant it for good, in order to bring it about as it is this day, to save many people alive." (Genesis 50:20)*

29

CHAPTER THREE

THE PRICE OF
THE CROSS

"Then He said to them all, "If anyone desires to come after Me, let him deny himself, and take up his cross [b]daily, and follow Me. For whoever desires to save his life will lose it, but whoever loses his life for My sake will save it." Luke 9: 23-24

At this point you may be thinking, this is supposed to be a book about the comfort of God, why are you writing about taking up your cross? It will all make sense in the end. The truth is that until we have a healthy understanding of suffering, we will label every form of inconvenience as suffering when it could well be part of the dealing of God in our lives. I am not in any way undermining the gravity of the pain and grief we experience even when we know it is part of the Lord's dealings. But I believe that when we know the source of the suffering and the purpose it is meant to accomplish in our lives, it makes it easier to endure knowing that it will yield a fruitful result in the end. Romans 5 renders it so beautifully,

Therefore, having been justified by faith, [a]we have peace

with God through our Lord Jesus Christ, through whom also we have access by faith into this grace in which we stand, and rejoice in hope of the glory of God. And not only that, but we also glory in tribulations, knowing that tribulation produces [b]perseverance; and perseverance, [c]character; and character, hope. Now hope does not disappoint, because the love of God has been poured out in our hearts by the Holy Spirit who was given to us.

Romans 5:1-5

WHY IS SUFFERING A NECESSARY PART OF CHRISTIANITY?

You may be asking, is this lady the leader of the "Pro-Suffering Movement", if there is such a thing, I am not, and I don't believe that believers should suffer unduly under personal demonic attacks. The Lord Jesus came to declare freedom and liberty from the domain of the enemy, that through his work on the cross, we might be free from the bondage of the enemy. Therefore, the only suffering a believer should go through is that which comes from persecution for the sake of the gospel and that which is sanction by God as a means of training the believer to bring him to a place of sonship, and maturity.

"He who sins is of the devil, for the devil has sinned from the beginning. For this purpose, the Son of God was manifested, that He might destroy the works of the devil."

1 John 3:8

The Spirit of the Lord is upon Me,
Because He has anointed Me

To preach the gospel to the poor;
He has sent Me [i]to heal the brokenhearted,
To proclaim liberty to the captives
And recovery of sight to the blind,
To set at liberty those who are [j]oppressed;
To proclaim the acceptable year of the Lord.

Luke 4:18-19

That is, the Lord does not desire for us to suffer under the dominion of the enemy. Yet He also understands that as we live in this corruptible body and as the enemy, the prince of this world is still working, there will be times that we have to endure some hardship and for every hardship that we go through, He gives us the grace to endure and overcome, and He compensates us for the sufferings that we go through. We will look into the justice and compensation system of God in the later chapters.

Now let us consider the different types of suffering and the purpose of suffering.

TYPES OF SUFFERING
- There is a suffering that leads to repentance 2 Cor 7:8-12
- Suffering that produces Godly character Romans 5:1-5
- Suffering for the purposes of God Acts 9:15-16
- Suffering as a result of sin Romans 6:23, James 1:13-15
- Suffering as a result of demonic attacks John 10:10

THE SUFFERING THAT LEADS TO REPENTANCE
Life is full of choices and in our journey, we make choices every day. Some choices lead us into the will of God and

other choices take us away from his intended purpose and these are the kinds of choices that lead us into sin and suffering. Many have faced the consequences of bad choices, in behaviours, finance, relationships, and others. But the Lord is always so faithful that even when we make choices that take us away from His will, he makes provision for us to return to Him and be saved.

Then He said: "A certain man had two sons. And the younger of them said to his father, 'Father, give me the portion of goods that falls to me.' So he divided to them his livelihood. And not many days after, the younger son gathered all together, journeyed to a far country, and there wasted his possessions with [d]prodigal living. But when he had spent all, there arose a severe famine in that land, and he began to be in want. Then he went and joined himself to a citizen of that country, and he sent him into his fields to feed swine. And he would gladly have filled his stomach with the [e]pods that the swine ate, and no one gave him anything.

"But when he came to himself, he said, 'How many of my father's hired servants have bread enough and to spare, and I perish with hunger! I will arise and go to my father, and will say to him, "Father, I have sinned against heaven and before you, 19 and I am no longer worthy to be called your son. Make me like one of your hired servants."

Luke 15:12-19

The parable of the prodigal son talks about the power of choice and the decision to repent. The years in the wilderness for this prodigal son started with a thought.

The enemy whispered in the hearing of the son to take his inheritance and go live out his life. Little did he know that the restrictions of His father's house were for his own safety. The enemy is still using this device of "freedom apart from righteousness" against many people. You may be in the faith yet be tempted to step out and experiment with the freedom in the world. You may be in a marriage and suddenly be enticed in the look and step outside of your marriage. This is the deception of the enemy. He will only show you the pleasure and the glamour you can pursue and never show you the consequences of your sin.

The prodigal son suffered many things while away from the safety of his father's house. He suffered and lost all the money He took with him until the came to himself. The enemy will never show you the other side of your decision until you find out the bitter end for yourself. You may be in a position where you are son far from the Lord, like the prodigal son, you may have also suffered a great loss. But in all of these, God is merciful and when we have a change of heart, He welcomes us and restores us to Himself, yet we must make the decision to return to Him in this midst of our suffering. Repentance is the beginning of change.

So repent (change your mind and purpose); turn around and return [to God], that your sins may be erased (blotted out, wiped clean), that times of refreshing (of recovering from the effects of heat, of [a]reviving with fresh air) may come from the presence of the Lord;

Acts 3:19

There is also a suffering that comes as a result of the discipline of the Lord. This was greatly experienced by King David after his affair with Bathsheba. Whenever we mingle with sin, it produces a separation between us and God, and the only way to rectify that is through the blood of Jesus and the work of His Grace. Yet the Lord chastens the ones He loves, to save us from continually sinning and walking away from the grace of God.

The love and the justice of God chastise us so He will not have to condemn us in Judgement. When your time of chastening comes, receive it with a good attitude.

For whom the Lord loves He chastens,
And scourges every son whom He receives."
If[a] you endure chastening, God deals with you as with
sons; for what son is there whom a father does not chasten?
But if you are without chastening, of which all have become
partakers, then you are illegitimate and not sons. Furthermore,
we have had human fathers who corrected us, and we paid
them respect.

Shall we not much more readily be in subjection to the Father
of spirits and live? For they indeed for a few days chastened
us as seemed best to them, but He for our profit, that we may
be partakers of His holiness. Now no [b]chastening seems to
be joyful for the present, but painful; nevertheless, afterward
it yields the peaceable fruit of righteousness to those who have
been trained by it.

Hebrews 12:6-11.

A SUFFERING THAT PRODUCES GODLY CHARACTER ROMANS 5:1-5

There is a suffering that develops a Godly character in the believer. This type of suffering does not necessarily mean that one has backslidden or walked away from the Lord. The believer can still be in Lord and yet be manifesting the deed of the flesh and carnality.

What do I mean by the deeds of the Flesh? The Apostle Paul called the church in Galatia to be mindful of their conduct towards each other and in his admonishment, he mentions specific things that he called the works of the flesh.

The acts of the flesh are obvious: sexual immorality, impurity and debauchery; idolatry and witchcraft; hatred, discord, jealousy, fits of rage, selfish ambition, dissensions, factions and envy; drunkenness, orgies, and the like. I warn you, as I did before, that those who live like this will not inherit the kingdom of God.

Galatians 5:19-23

Now some believers take the acts or the deeds of the flesh lightly, on the premise that a person can be a believer and still be indulging in these acts. The danger of such thinking is that they omit the part that says, "that those who live like this will not inherit the kingdom of God" and again in Revelations, the Lord specifically says that:

But the cowardly, the unbelieving, the vile, the murderers, the sexually immoral, those who practice magic arts, the idolaters and all liars—they will be consigned to the fiery lake of burning sulfur. This is the second death.

Revelations 21:8

The Apostle Paul, knowing the consequences and the result of living in the flesh, called out the Galatian Church to put to death the works of the flesh. This admonishing was not only for the Galatian Church but for all believers. The suffering of training ourselves unto Godliness is far less than the punishment of living an undisciplined and ungodly lifestyle that will lead you to eternal condemnation.

Knowing therefore the terror of the Lord, we persuade men; but we are made manifest unto God; and I trust also are made manifest in your consciences.

2 Corinthians 5:11-21

Mortify therefore your members which are upon the earth; fornication, uncleanness, inordinate affection, evil concupiscence, and covetousness, which is idolatry: For which things' sake the wrath of God cometh on the children of disobedience.

Colossians 3:5-11

How then do we put the deeds of the flesh? Let us consider the directives in **Romans 5:1-5**

Therefore, having been justified by faith, [a]we have peace with God through our Lord Jesus Christ, 2 through whom also we have access by faith into this grace in which we stand, and rejoice in hope of the glory of God. 3 And not only that, but we also glory in tribulations, knowing that tribulation produces [b]perseverance; 4 and perseverance, [c]character;

and character, hope. 5 Now hope does not disappoint, because
the love of God has been poured out in our hearts by the Holy
Spirit who was given to us.

HOW DO WE WORK THIS OUT IN OUR DAILY LIVES?

I work in the Human Resource Sector as a matter of profession
and about 3 years ago I registered a recruitment business
that I have been working on aside my full-time HR position.
In the past 6 years, I have been living between Canada and
the United Kingdom. In 2018, I returned to Canada due to
my marriage ending and had to take various contract HR
positions as my business had not yielded any profit yet.
One of the employers that I worked with was quite unjust
in their dealing with their employees. Without going into
much detail about the compensation from this company, I
will say this; they presented what seemed like an attractive
compensation system but offered a different pay-out once
you were in the company. As a well-performing recruiter
and account manager with my own side business, there were
times when going after this employer's clients seemed like a
fair payback for the financial injustice I was going through
with this employer. But the Lord put a restraining order on
me and reminded me that as a believer, I could not operate
under the world's system and expect the Lord to bless it.
At the same time, He would not let me leave the company
before the time he had apportioned for me to be there.

The Lord said to me He will not bless what I take out of
corruption and it was not time to leave the company either.
And from the moment, I made a decision that no matter
what inequity I faced at that workplace, I would not reach

out on behalf of my company to any of the clients I bought to this lady's company as I was paid to do the job and reaching out to them after hours equates stealing and I would not let the wrong done to me cause me to do wrong. Yet I was still strong on finding another position and leaving the company.

Oh, I how fought with the Lord. I was like 'it is one thing for me not to seek revenge for the employment inequity and another thing not to seek employment elsewhere'. I kept on applying for other jobs, but the Lord would not open the door. I would have interviews and would seem to go well but nothing would come out of it. I was anxious because I had applied to attend a Bible College in the U. K and needed to save some money for my tuition, accommodation, and plane ticket. This was a trying time for me. I had already told my church I would be going to the bible college and people kept asking me when are you leaving? And I would respond, very soon. Meanwhile, I needed a minimum of $10000 to pay for my tuition, accommodation, and other personal expense and I had about $500 in savings.

People that did not want me to go to this Bible school were banking on me not getting the funds to go and staying back in Canada. Yet I kept working on my business after hours, reaching out to companies in different industries and making sure I did not reach out to any company that was affiliated with my employer. Finally, 3 weeks before the school would start, I got a contract from a company I had applied to work with 2 years prior, and they did not hire me and gave the position to another candidate. Somehow, I got the courage to reach out to them regarding my personal recruitment company and they had an urgent need for a Project Estimator in the Demolition Industry. They hired my candidate a week before the start of the Bible College and I received a cheque of $14,000, the very first successful and profitable contract my company had earned after 3 years of being in business.

Now, why do I share this story? Through this experience, the Lord thought me various lessons and strengthened my integrity. I thought I had integrity until it was tested and I was cheated and treated unfairly which in the world's view, would be a perfect justification to lose my integrity and act in revenge, but the Lord helped me to persevere in character. Now, my integrity is strengthened not only when things are normal but especially when I am tried.

Secondly, I learned to trust God for my provision. I knew God was calling to attend the Bible college and I resolved not to borrow to pay for my tuition. I wanted to exercise my faith to receive from God and truly, my faith was stretched and, in the end, He made a way.

Lastly, there were many that discouraged me from taking the journey to go to the Bible college, yet I knew I heard God and it was in His will for me to go to the Bible College. I learnt in that situation to obey the voice of God over the influence of man.

This situation to me is an example of perseverance resulting in character, and character giving birth to hope, knowing that If I follow the leading of the Holy Spirit and obey the word of God, He will not fail me, He will always comfort and provide.

For others, they may need to overcome in other areas such as sexual purity, overcoming the urge to gossip, overcoming a bad attitude, or whatever area the Lord lays his hands on in your life. Give yourself to suffering in the dealings of God. For through His dealings, He works in us His nature, that is the nature of Christ.

For the time being no discipline brings joy, but seems sad and painful; yet to those who have been trained by it, afterwards it yields the peaceful fruit of righteousness [right standing with God and a lifestyle and attitude that seeks conformity to God's will and purpose. Hebrews 12:11

SUFFERING THAT FOR THE PURPOSES OF GOD
ACTS 9:15-16

But the Lord said to him, "Go, for this man is a [deliberately] chosen instrument of Mine, to bear My name before the Gentiles and kings and the sons of Israel; 16 for I will make clear to him how much he must suffer and endure for My name's sake."

Acts 9:15-16

Besides the Lord Jesus Christ, we can safely say there is no one who suffered so much for the sake of the Gospel like the Apostle Paul. Indeed, his calling was one that came packaged with suffering and grief. For the sake of his mission to spread the gospel to the gentiles, the Apostle Paul experienced great difficulty in every city that he endeavoured to penetrate with the gospel.

Paul experienced great hostility from the elite, that is the

42

Pharisees, and the Sanhedrin for deserting them for the faith he once persecuted. He gives an account of his zeal in Galatians.

For you have heard of my former conduct in Judaism, how I persecuted the church of God beyond measure and tried to destroy it. And I advanced in Judaism beyond many of my contemporaries in my own nation, being more exceedingly zealous for the traditions of my fathers.

Galatians 1:13-14

On the other hand, he faced rejection from the believers; for some could not believe that the one who once persecuted the faith was converted and preaching the gospel.

Afterward I went into the regions of Syria and Cilicia. And I was unknown by face to the churches of Judea which were in Christ. But they were hearing only, "He who formerly persecuted us now preaches the faith which he once tried to destroy." And they glorified God in me.

Galatians 1:22-24

In his letter to the Corinthians, the Apostle Paul responded to the contentions in the church concerning his apostleship, his many sufferings for the sake of the gospel.

Are they Hebrews? So am I. Are they Israelites? So am I. Are they the seed of Abraham? So am I. Are they ministers of Christ?—I speak as a fool—I am more: in labours more abundant, in stripes above measure, in prisons more frequently, in deaths often.

From the Jews five times I received forty stripes minus one. Three times I was beaten with rods; once I was stoned; three times I was shipwrecked; a night and a day I have been in the deep; in journeys often, in perils of waters, in perils of robbers, in perils of my own countrymen, in perils of the Gentiles, in perils in the city, in perils in the wilderness, in perils in the sea, in perils among false brethren; in weariness and toil, in sleeplessness often, in hunger and thirst, in fasting often, in cold and nakedness—besides the other things, what comes upon me daily: my deep concern for all the churches. Who is weak, and I am not weak? Who is made to stumble, and I do not burn with indignation?

2 Corinthians 11:22-23

Besides all the contentions and hardships, he faced from the authorities, the communities he ministered to, and some believers in Jerusalem, he faced desertion and betrayal from some of his ministry co-labourers.

Be diligent to come to me quickly; for Demas has forsaken me, having loved this present world, and has departed for Thessalonica—Crescens for Galatia, Titus for Dalmatia. Only Luke is with me. Get Mark and bring him with you, for he is useful to me for ministry. And Tychicus I have sent to Ephesus. Bring the cloak that I left with Carpus at Troas when you come—and the books, especially the parchments.

Alexander the coppersmith did me much harm. May the Lord repay him according to his works. You also must beware of him, for he has greatly resisted our words.

At my first defense no one stood with me, but all forsook me.
May it not be charged against them.The Lord Is Faithful.
But the Lord stood with me and strengthened me, so that the
message might be preached fully through me, and that all the
Gentiles might hear. Also, I was delivered out of the mouth of
the lion. And the Lord will deliver me from every evil work
and preserve me for His heavenly kingdom. To Him be glory
forever and ever. Amen!

2 Timothy 4:9-13

The Apostle Paul in all of his sufferings still stayed focused
on his call and contributed 13 books out of the 27 books of
the new testament. That is, the will of God can lead you into
great suffering yet in all of the sufferings, His will is perfected
in us.

Acts 12 gives an account of the Herod's tyranny claiming the
life of believers including the Apostle James and his desire
to kill the Apostle Peter which was thwarted through the
prayers of the saints. We cannot treat the subject of suffering
for the purposes of God without considering the man who
made it all possible for man to receive salvation, the Lord
Jesus Christ. Hundreds of years before His birth, the Prophet
Isaiah prophesied about His birth in Isaiah 9 and about his
life, ministry, and death in Isaiah 53. He called Him the
suffering servant.

He is despised and [d]rejected by men,
A Man of [e]sorrows and acquainted with [f]grief.
And we hid, as it were, our faces from Him;
He was despised, and we did not esteem Him.

Surely He has borne our [g]griefs
And carried our [h]sorrows;
Yet we [i]esteemed Him stricken,
[j]Smitten by God, and afflicted.
But He was wounded[k] for our transgressions,
He was [l]bruised for our iniquities;
The chastisement for our peace was upon Him,
And by His stripes[m] we are healed.
All we like sheep have gone astray;
We have turned, every one, to his own way;
And the Lord [n]has laid on Him the iniquity of us all…
Yet it pleased the Lord to [q]bruise Him;
He has put Him to grief.

Jesus qualifies to be our perfect comforter because He can identify with our sorrows. The prophet Isaiah described Him as a Man of Sorrows and acquainted with [f]grief.

CHAPTER FOUR

THE GRIEVER'S CRY

WHY DO WE CRY?

We cry when we are in pain when we have lost something or have experienced a bitter experience. The Bible contains many accounts of people crying out to God for mercy and help. The cry of the wounded comes in many forms, some cry by isolating themselves, some in anger, and others cry by "letting loose", and yet others cry by seeking vengeance. But the cry that the Lord is looking to hear from us is the cry for mercy and help. The Lord loves us so much that He hurts when we hurt. Picture a good father with a child who has been deeply wounded and weeping uncontrollably. What would a good father do in a situation like this? A good father would sit with the child and comfort them. God is much more than a good father. David in Psalm 34, David said,

The righteous cry out, and the Lord hears them; he delivers them from all their troubles. The Lord is close to the broken-hearted and saves those who are crushed in spirit."

Psalm 34:17-18

Many cry, but they cry in the wrong way and to the wrong people.

CRYING IN ANGER

There is a saying that "Anger is love that is disappointed, and behind every anger is a root of pain ". Many angry people are people who once cared about a situation, a thing, or a person and have somehow been wounded by various issues and are crying out in anger. Some are angry at themselves, some are angry at God, some at their parents, some at their offenders, others are angry and frustrated by life itself. While they may have reasons to justify their anger, their anger only deepens their wounds and creates other problems in their lives. Many wound themselves by their anger.

For the wrath of man does not produce the righteousness of God.

James 1:20

NEGATIVE EFFECTS OF ANGER

Anger is the causal effect behind many issues, diseases, and sickness. Governments direct immerse resources toward dealing the challenges and the effects of anger, through the healthcare department, the courts and judiciary systems, and other social interventions. It is also the cause of many issues such as challenges in relationships, marriages, work, and many other areas. Studies show that anger has been the main cause of violence, physical and emotional abuse. Anger has caused many people to walk away and lose opportunities, many homes have been wrecked because of anger. Lives have been lost and opportunities destroyed by the beast of anger.

48

I can say that my own home was wrecked because of anger. My partner and I had misunderstandings on things that were really insignificant in many respects, but anger took over and sound reasoning could not prevail. Some express their anger explosively and others repress their anger. My Aunt once said; anger makes you think and behave like a fool. But to the person who is wounded, anger becomes their defence.

An angry person exhibits symptoms of bitterness, rage, bad attitude, and even fear. I have seen people who have held on to anger and have been bleeding in many situations instead of seeking healing. One of the worst pains that I have endured is witnessing a person close to me being completely consumed by anger and living all their live through the lens of anger and bitterness instead of giving it over to God. Angry people make many mistakes, walk in dishonour, damaging many relationships that could have been a blessing to them all because they are holding on to their hurt. Yet the Lord waits with arms wide open to be gracious and to heal.

Therefore, the Lord will wait, that He may be gracious to you; And therefore, He will be exalted, that He may have mercy on you. For the Lord is a God of justice; Blessed are all those who wait for Him.

Isaiah 30: 18

The enemy delights in attaching himself to our weaknesses and our mistakes. The Apostle Paul warns believers about anger giving place to the enemy. He uses our weaknesses to gain an advantage over us.

"In your anger do not sin"[a]: Do not let the sun go down while you are still angry. nor give [g]place to the devil."

Ephesians 4: 26-27

CRYING IN ISOLATING

"No one ever told me that grief felt so much like fear."
C.S. Lewis, A Grief Observed.

Pain has the ability to make us feel ashamed and fearful. This fear and shame often result in people isolating themselves from their loved ones in hopes of protecting their "shame" and keep from getting hurt again.

Since the fall, man has been hiding anytime he feels hurt and ashamed. Adam and his wife, Eve, tried to hide from God when they discovered their nakedness. But God always calls us out to Himself. Let's take a look into the dialog between God and man when man hid from the presence of God.

And they heard the [c]sound of the Lord God walking in the garden in the [d]cool of the day, and Adam and his wife hid themselves from the presence of the Lord God among the trees of the garden.

Then the Lord God called to Adam and said to him, "Where are you?" So he said, "I heard Your voice in the garden, and I was afraid because I was naked; and I hid myself." And He said, "Who told you that you were naked? Have you eaten from the tree of which I commanded you that you should not eat?"

Galatians 3:8-11

Why did Adam hide from God? He hid because he knew he had disobeyed God and there was an impending judgement that awaited him. Many of us still live in that mindset when we do wrong or when we are wronged. We hide for the fear of judgement, we hide to keep ourselves from being hurt again, we hide from our "nakedness".

The Apostle Paul talks about the veil that covered the reading of the old testament. That is, Adam hid from God because He anticipated the judgement of God. However, in this dispensation of Grace, we are beckoned to come into the presence of God to find mercy for our unrighteous dealings and grace for our troubles.

Therefore, since we have such hope, we use great boldness of speech—unlike Moses, who put a veil over his face so that the children of Israel could not look steadily at the end of what was passing away. But their minds were blinded. For until this day the same veil remains unlifted in the reading of the Old Testament, because the veil is taken away in Christ. But even to this day, when Moses is read, a veil lies on their heart. Nevertheless when one turns to the Lord, the veil is taken away. Now the Lord is the Spirit; and where the Spirit of the Lord is, there is liberty. But we all, with unveiled face, beholding as in a mirror the glory of the Lord, are being transformed into the same image from glory to glory, just as [b]by the Spirit of the Lord.

2 Corinthians 3:12-18

Notice the scripture says, **"Nevertheless when one turns to the Lord, the veil is taken away. Now the Lord is the Spirit;**

and where the Spirit of the Lord is, there is liberty".

In our sorrow, we ought to turn to the Lord and not run from Him. I understand that sometimes, based on the situation you may have encountered, you may need to take some time away from the situation and from people to heal and be made whole. There should be time you take away from toxic people and may need a change of environment or location, yet the Lord calls us to turn to Him. In our pain, we need the comfort and wisdom of God sometimes that comes through Godly people who can speak healing into our lives. Yes, you may sometimes need to step away from the crowd but it is imperative to stay connected with people who can encourage, correct, edify, and strengthen us and nurse you back to good health, emotionally, spiritually, and physically. There are times that God may lead you to step away from the crowd into His Presence.

Personally, I'm writing this book in a sabbatical season, where I've stepped away from all that is common to me, stepped away from the life I knew, to be in the presence of God to be instructed, healed, comforted, and made whole. After my divorce, I felt the need to step away from all that was familiar to a place where I can be alone with God. I did this 2 years after my divorce. That is, in the heat of the battle, I relied on the support of my family and loved ones who gave me godly counsel, supported, comforted me. I could not have survived those difficult moments without the help, and love of Godly influences in my life. But while I had a strong support system, I felt the need to also be alone with God for some time and truly this sabbatical has been a blessing to me in many ways.

THE ENEMY'S ISOLATION STRATEGY

A man who isolates himself seeks his own desire; He rages against all wise judgment.

Proverbs 18:1

There is common knowledge that the enemy likes to divide and conquer. That is, like a predator, he waits and lurks around to see who is vulnerable so he might devour them. The devil does not play fair. He is cold, mean, wicked, and evil. He attacks you the most when you are in the place of vulnerability, and there is no greater vulnerability than when are wounded and alone.

Be sober, be vigilant; because your adversary the devil, as a roaring lion, walketh about, seeking whom he may devour: Whom resist steadfast in the faith, knowing that the same afflictions are accomplished in your brethren that are in the world.

1 Peter 5:8-9

The enemy's strategy is to get you alone in a place where he can easily manipulate, control, and get you to compromise. Being in isolation is dangerous when you are wounded. He isolates people in fear and shame, but God calls us into His body, to be a part of His family. When wounded, you may feel unloved, rejected, defeated, and judged. He whispers these thoughts in your head to keep you from embracing the love and support of others. This he does to keep your heart rooted in bitterness, and out of such a heart, he then controls your life and sways you from the truth of the word of God.

Some people out of bitterness have left their place of covering, rejected the love and support they could have received from others, and abandoned godly connections but God calls us into the beloved.

..having predestined us to adoption as sons by Jesus Christ to Himself, according to the good pleasure of His will, 6 to the praise of the glory of His grace, by which He [a]made us accepted in the Beloved.

Ephesians 1:5-7

When the news of my divorce became "public" in my circles, I felt ashamed, hurt, and fearful of the judgement of people. What will people say? And yes, many said a lot. I had instances where a young lady totally smirked in my face when she saw me. I was so shocked that I just looked at her and shook my head and said this too shall pass. I knew at that moment that while she may represent a few insensitive people, she was not a representation of the father's heart towards me. So I kept going to church, I kept singing and doing all I needed to do.

The enemy sure gave me suggestions on how to isolate myself in the midst of my pain. He told me to leave the church, don't talk to anyone because people are rejoicing over the fall of the little "Christian girl". And he used some church members to justify his suggestions for me to leave the church.

I remember being put on a program with one of the branches as a guest music minister for a 4-day program. I went for a rehearsal and was on my way the next day for another rehearsal. I got a call from the Pastor that they had cancelled my ministration appointment and I asked why to which he said, 'I can't say much but it is due to your divorce' to which I replied '...but you knew my husband had divorced me before you invited me for the program?'.

Another time I ministered at women's program and after the ministration, a report came back to me indicating the local Pastor was not happy about the organizing leader having me on the program all because I was a victim of a divorce. The victim was being victimized again. Thankfully, I knew that the church's treatment of me was not an indication that God had rejected me.

Sometimes, church leaders can get it wrong and it only goes to prove their humanity, after all they are human beings who have received the grace to shepherd God's people and they sometimes get it wrong. We must also show patience and forgiveness towards them and not fight them when they miss it. I decided not to be offended or hold bitterness against anyone, I brought it before the Lord and prayed that the Lord would handle the situation as best as He pleases. Not long, after that, the same Pastor who was not happy with the leader for having me on the program came to me and said he would reserve a ministration spot for me every month, to which he did and I thank him that he did harden his heart towards me but allowed the Lord to make right what he got wrong. God knows how to correct situations when we are wronged.

God has promised his presence to anyone who will embrace

him. You are never alone and never without comfort. His Holy Spirit is there to heal and to comfort. Do not let the enemy keep you in isolation, embrace the love of God, and embrace the beloved. Had I isolated myself at that time, I would have still been bitter and angry, blaming all other people and having problems with the leaders, but it took the chance to speak to some of them when the opportunity came to explain my side of things and to let them know the stories that was made up but me were not true without maliciously destroying my ex-husband. But I kept on singing Sunday after Sunday when given the chance, Isang my heart out when I got the chance to minister, I danced in the presence of God and man and continued fellowshipping with the beloved.

The difference between my current sabbatical and the enemy's proposed Isolation is that in my current time away, I went away to be with the Lord at the Bible College, and being here has been a blessing as it has helped me redefine my purpose, spend time with God and be with other spirit-filled students from the college. I have found wholeness and renewed purpose. The Lord has truly removed all anger and bitterness from my heart and completely broken the spirit of fear and the lack of trust from my heart. I can say I am a completely different woman. I do not live from my wounds as I have been healed and I do not live from the place of fear. I spend my time in the presence of God interceding for others, even those who caused me so much pain, whereas isolating myself in pain would have prolonged my healing and caused me to be bitter.

LETTING LOOSE

When people do not accept divine guidance, they run wild. But whoever obeys the law is joyful.

Proverbs 29:18

Grief can make people lose sight of what is important. When we are grieving, the potential of having a narrow vision of life increases. Most people cannot see a way out or cannot imagine the possibility of healing and seeing an end to their time of sorrow. Thus, grievers in certain situations end their lives through suicide or end their lives just living for the moment, aimless and purposeless. In the season of grieve, many cast off any restraints. According to the World Health Organization, low income countries on average have less suicide rates as compared to high income countries due to mental health, (WHO). This could be attributed to the fact that low income countries tend to have a strong community support system that helps and engages people, keeping them from isolation and depression while developed and wealthy countries are more centred on individuality and independence and as such, people tend to live more in isolation from others, contributing to greater anxiety and mental health issues.

Many hurt people try to fill the void of pain in their heart by living promiscuous, wild party lifestyle only to find their hearts emptier than before and when the emptiness begins to drown their soul, they end their lives by committing suicide or getting in trouble with the law.

The commandment of God is to protect us and not to harm

us. For us believers, pain must not be a reason for living a wild life. We must obey the word of God in good seasons and in bad seasons. There is something that I call the "deception of pain". This occurs when the enemy deceives us with a sense of entitlement to live life on our own terms. When are wronged, there is the tendency to think and live entitled as if God and the world owes us something? This mindset can lead people to become vengeful, violent, wild, and living a lifestyle that leads to destruction. However, when in our pain we remember that we live in a falling world and there is grace and hope in God, we are able to live soberly, submitting ourselves under the guidance and the authority of the Holy Spirit, who leads us into healing and wholeness.

You may be going through a time of pain and difficulty now and you may be tempted to rebel but that is the deception of the enemy. He wants to lead you into more hardship and pain, and worse, keep you in eternity away from God. The love of God is deeper felt even in pain. Obedience to God even when wronged leads to healing and restoration.

The law of the Lord is perfect, [e]converting the soul;
The testimony of the Lord is sure, making wise the simple;
The statutes of the Lord are right, rejoicing the heart;
The commandment of the Lord is pure, enlightening the eyes;
The fear of the Lord is clean, enduring forever;
The judgments of the Lord are true and righteous altogether.
More to be desired are they than gold,
Yea, than much fine gold;
Sweeter also than honey and the [f]honeycomb.
Moreover by them Your servant is warned,

And in keeping them there is great reward.

Psalm 19:7-14

THE CRY FOR VENGEANCE

The Psalms are filled with a cry of vengeance and restitution. Nothing satisfies the heart of the unrenewed man than to see their desire on their enemies. King David was one such character who faced many adversaries and was expressive about his pain and anguish.

Vindicate me, O God,
And plead my cause against an ungodly nation;
Oh, deliver me from the deceitful and unjust man!
For You are the God of my strength;
Why do You cast me off?
Why do I go mourning because of the oppression of the enemy?

Psalm 43:1-2

The Old Testament is filled with many of these cries, as people pour out their hearts to God in search of a solution, vindication, and vengeance for their enemies. Of a truth, the old testament God was a God of vengeance as His dealing with men was under the law. Hence, He took literal vengeance of the adversaries of His people. Yet in the New Testament era, God's system of restitution is much different than that of the old testament.

The finished work of Christ on the cross took away the wrath of God towards man not only as it relates to salvation but also as to how God deals with human relationships. In the New Testament, The Lord Jesus and the Apostles admonished us

59

as to how to handle conflicts and how to handle offenses. In dealings with conflict, hurt, loss, and grief, It is imperative to understand the heart and the character of God concerning these matters. Understanding the heart of God towards man expediates our healing, gives us an understanding of the importance of forgiveness and helps us to seek reconciliation instead of vengeance. The heart of God is for reconciliation.

Now all things are of God, who has reconciled us to Himself through Jesus Christ, and has given us the ministry of reconciliation, 19 that is, that God was in Christ reconciling the world to Himself, not [d]imputing their trespasses to them, and has committed to us the word of reconciliation.

2 Corinthians 5:19

Repay no one evil for evil. Have[e] regard for good things in the sight of all men. 18 If it is possible, as much as depends on you, live peaceably with all men. Beloved, do not avenge yourselves, but rather give place to wrath; for it is written, "Vengeance is Mine, I will repay," says the Lord. Therefore

"If your enemy is hungry, feed him;
If he is thirsty, give him a drink;
For in so doing you will heap coals of fire on his head."
Do not be overcome by evil but overcome evil with good.

Romans 12:17-21

While our flesh may be crying for blood when we are wronged, we must remember that God honours those who show mercy. He is a God who shows mercy and makes allowances for the shortcomings of others and we must in our walk with God and our dealing with our fellow human beings, endeavour to show mercy. It is not always easy but God is gracious. If we are willing, He will grant us the grace. Mercy triumphs over judgement.

CHAPTER FIVE

THE ATTACK ON YOUR NAME AND IDENTITY

WHO ARE YOU?

This is a question many are struggling to answer, and this is the very thing that the enemy is fighting to keep us from knowing. Knowing your identity answers so many questions of your life and is one of the paramount keys to finding your place in life. When you successfully answer the question of identity, you can then define your:

- Purpose (Gifts, Talent, Scope of Influence)
- Your Areas of Strength and Weaknesses
- Your Community and Tribe

YOUR IDENTITY: WHO ARE YOU?

While we may have many imposed and earned identities, there are two primary sources from which we get or perceive our identity. I consider these the core source of identity. These are, the families we are born and raised into and for us believers, our ultimate identity comes from our relationship with the Lord Jesus. I call these our earthly and heavenly identities. We get our earthly identity at birth from the last name we carry and our heavenly identity the day we decided to make Jesus our Lord and saviour.

OUR EARTHLY IDENTITY

Our earthly identities are inherited and shaped by the families we are born into. When we take a family name, much can be said about the people that bear that last name and within that family. Everyone in the family has their unique identities based on their form, uniqueness, gifts, and talents. Our earthly identity is usually based on the very things with which we can be identified, the little identifiers. For this reason, our earthly identities can be fractured. We will consider this later.

The Bible makes it clear that a child or person's identity is first given by their father and this is why the presence of a father is so paramount in forming our identity and the absence of a father is greatly felt in most cases so negatively. This truth is the underlying factor as to why many people feel displaced, rejected, and unwanted. We often talk about the importance of the father in carving the identity of the children, the question is what that is practically like.

Let's consider the text from Genesis 49.

And JACOB CALLED his sons AND SAID, "GATHER together, THAT I MAY tell you WHAT SHALL BEFALL you in the LAST DAYS:

"GATHER together AND HEAR, you sons of JACOB, And listen to ISRAEL your FATHER.

"Reuben, you are my firstborn,
My might AND the beginning of my strength,
The excellency of dignity AND the excellency of power.

UNSTABLE AS WATER, you SHALL not excel, BECAUSE you went up to your FATHER's bed; Then you defiled it—He went up to my couch.

"Simeon AND Levi are brothers;
Instruments of [A]CRUELTY are in their dwelling PLACE.
Let not my soul enter their council;
Let not my honor be united to their ASSEMBLY; For in their ANGER they slew A MAN,

And in their self-will they [B]HAMSTRUNG AN ox. Cursed be their ANGER, for it is fierce;
And their WRATH, for it is cruel! I will divide them in JACOB And SCATTER them in ISRAEL.

"JUDAH, you are he whom your brothers SHALL PRAISE; Your HAND SHALL be on the neck of your enemies; Your FATHER's children SHALL bow down before you.
JUDAH is A lion's whelp;

From the prey, my son, you HAVE gone up. He [c]bows down, he lies down AS A lion; And AS A lion, who SHALL rouse him?

The [d]scepter SHALL not DEPART from JUDAH, Nor A LAWGIVER from between his feet,
Until Shiloh comes;

And to Him SHALL be the obedience of the people. Binding his donkey to the vine,
And his donkey's colt to the choice vine,
He WASHED his GARMENTS in wine,
And his clothes in the blood of GRAPES. His eyes ARe DARKER THAN wine,
And his teeth whiter THAN milk.

"Zebulun SHALL dwell by the HAVEN of the SEA; He SHALL become A HAVEN for ships,
And his border SHALL ADJOIN Sidon.

"ISSACHAR is A STRong donkey, Lying down between two burdens; He SAW THAT rest WAS good,
And THAT the LAND WAS PLEASANT;
He bowed his shoulder to BEAR A burden, And BECAME A BAND of SLAVES.

"DAN SHALL judge his people As one of the tribes of ISRAEL. DAN SHALL be A SERPENT by the WAY, A viper by the PATH, THAT bites the horse's heels
So THAT its rider SHALL FALL BACKWARD.
I HAVE WAITED for your SALVATION, O Lord!

"GAD,[E] A troop SHALL [F]TRAMP upon him, But he SHALL triumph AT LAST.
"BrEAD from Asher SHALL be rich, And he SHALL yield ROYAL DAINTIES.

"NAPHTALI is A deer let loose; He uses BEAUTIFUL words.

"Joseph is A fruitful bough, A fruitful bough by A well;
His BRANCHES run over the WALL.
The ARchers HAVE bitterly grieved him, Shot AT him AND
HATED him.
But his bow rEMAINED in strength,
And the ARMS of his HANDS were [G]MADE strong

By the HANDS of the Mighty God of JACOB
(From there is the Shepherd, the Stone of ISRAEL), By the
God of your FATHER who will help you, And by the Almighty
who will bless you
With blessings of HEAVEN ABOVE, Blessings of the deep
THAT lies BENEATH, Blessings of the BREASTS AND of the
womb. The blessings of your FATHER

HAVE excelled the blessings of my ANCESTORS, Up to the
utmost bound of the EVERLASTING hills. They SHALL be on
the HEAD of Joseph,
And on the crown of the HEAD of him who WAS SEPARATE
from his brothers.

"BENJAMIN is A RAVENOUS wolf;
In the morning he SHALL devour the prey, And AT night he
SHALL divide the spoil."

All these are the twelve tribes of ISRAEL, AND this is
WHAT their FATHER spoke to them. And he blessed them; he
blessed EACH one according to his own blessing.

In this passage, we see Jacob speaking a blessing and, in some
instances, curses over His children. Now, this was at the time

that his children were grown and had various experiences yet he spoke over their lives to initiate them into the next phase of their lives. His words were a mixture of who they had been in the past and what he could perceive and wish for in their future.

Let's examine his words over 3 of his sons. Reuben, Judah, and Joseph. Genesis 49:1-4

REUBEN
"Reuben, you are my firstborn,
My might AND the beginning of my strength,
The excellency of dignity AND the excellency of power. 4
UNSTABLE AS WATER, you SHALL not excel,
BECAUSE you went up to your FATHER's bed; Then you defiled it—
He went up to my couch.

According to this text, Jacob calls Reuben his first son and his might, the beginning of his strength, the excellency of dignity and power. Thus, Reuben's identity was to be a person of excellence, strength, dignity, might, and power. That is a very powerful destiny. Yet Jacob added what seemed to be a curse on Reuben's destiny because of his mistake of having a sexual affair with his father's mistress.

And it HAPPENED, when ISRAEL dwelt in THAT LAND, THAT Reuben went AND LAY with BILHAH his FATHER's concubine; AND ISRAEL HEARD ABOUT it.
Genesis 35:22

There are two things to be noted here. That is, we must be careful how we deal with our biological and spiritual fathers. I understand that some of us may have experienced the pain of an imperfect father, an absent father, an ungodly father, and sometimes an outright wicked and mean father. But the principles of God remain the same across the board even when we are dealing with fathers who may have wounded us or walked out on us. The first step to show honour to our earthly fathers who may have wounded us, is to forgive them. It is impossible to honour a person you have not forgiven.

In the case of Reuben, his initial identity was of strength, excellence, and power. Yet his father imposed another identity on him based on his failures and weaknesses.

With God, however, there is always redemption for our lives and destinies. The curse on Reuben's bloodline was redeemed and reversed by Moses years later and restored the dignity and strength of Reuben. There are many ways that God redeems our lives from the curses placed on our life. In the case of Reuben, we see God redeeming the curse on him in Deuteronomy 33. Moses, who was a leader of God's people Israel and a representation of a father, pronounced blessings on the tribe of Israel before his death and in it, He reversed the curse placed on the tribe of Reuben.

"Let Reuben live, AND not die, Nor let his men be few."
Deuteronomy 33: 6

Because of the curse that was placed on Reuben's life, generations after him were suffering and were not living long. And Moses, the leader of Israel, representing the father's authority, had to reverse the curse by speaking positively about the time of Reuben and declaring long life and longevity over the tribe of Reuben.

There are many who do not believe in generational curses as believers. I do understand where the confusion is for such people. Having the understanding that the death and resurrection of Jesus Christ has redeemed us from the curse of sin, one argues that where then lies the power of generational curses. There is a British Preacher who has gone on to be with the Lord and who was an authoritative voice on the matter of curses and generational curses, Derek Prince. You can look up his books on Amazon and his teachings on youtube.

The question is; can a born-again Christian be under a generational curse? The answer is yes and no. This is why in everything that Christ did for us, He completed and finished yet the appropriation of it is based on our knowledge of what the Lord Jesus has done through prayer. The enemy knows that he is a defeated foe yet that does not stop him from constantly harassing the people of God. That is why Jesus admonished us to always watch and pray. The Apostle Paul also admonished us to pray without ceasing.

There are spiritual legalities governing some spiritual issues that we must be aware of through the inspiration of the Holy Spirit. This is why every believer must strive to speak in tongues and exercise discernment. Sometimes, some people in our bloodline may make being involved in the occult or have covenanted with the enemy and grant the enemy the legal right to dominate specific areas of the lives of individuals in their bloodline. The enemy will in turn enforce his dominance on the people in the bloodline but it takes a person who has yielded to God and knows their rights in God's kingdom to enforce the finished work of Christ and break the demonic dominance in the bloodline.

That is, for Reuben, Moses representing the authority in Israel enforced his deliverance by reversing the curse. From that time forth, not only did the men of Reuben excel but they lived and multiplied as well. The ultimate redemption of our identity and destiny is when we find ourselves in Christ, the father who delivers us and gives us new identities.

THE CASE OF JUDAH

"JUDAH, you are he whom your brothers SHALL PRAISE; Your HAND SHALL be on the neck of your enemies; Your FATHER's children SHALL bow down before you. JUDAH is A lion's whelp;

From the prey, my son, you HAVE gone up. He [c]bows down, he lies down AS A lion; And AS A lion, who SHALL rouse him? The [d]scepter SHALL not DEPART from JUDAH, Nor A LAWGIVER from between his feet, Until Shiloh comes;

And to Him SHALL be the obedience of the people. Binding his donkey to the vine, And his donkey's colt to the choice vine, He WASHED his

GARMENTS in wine,
And his clothes in the blood of GRAPES. His eyes ARe
DARKER THAN wine,
And his teeth whiter THAN milk

Genesis 49:8-11

Jacob's words established Judah as an authority and ruler amongst his brethren and true to these words, the tribe of Judah is the tribe of King David, the greatest earthly King in Israel, and out of the lineage of the tribe of Judah came the Lord Jesus Christ. The Lord God made a promise to David that He would build him a house and establish his throne forever.

Moreover I will APPOINT A PLACE for My people ISRAEL,
AND will PLANT them, THAT they MAY dwell in A PLACE
of their own AND move no more; nor SHALL the sons of
wickedness oppress them ANYMORe, AS previously, since
the time THAT I COMMANDED judges to be over My people
ISRAEL. Also, I will subdue ALL your enemies. Furthermore I
tell you THAT the Lord will build you A [c]house.

And it SHALL be, when your DAYS ARe fulfilled, when you
must [d]go to be with your FATHERS, THAT I will set up
your seed AFTER you, who will be of your sons; AND I will
ESTABLISH his kingdom. He SHALL build Me A house, AND
I will ESTABLISH his throne forever. I will be his FATHER,
AND he SHALL be My son; AND I will not TAKE My mercy
AWAY from him, AS I took it from him who WAS before you.
And I will ESTABLISH him in My house AND in My kingdom
forever; AND his throne SHALL be ESTABLISHED forever."

1 Chronicles 17:9-14

This word of promise was fulfilled in the rule and reign of the Lord Jesus who was from the line of Judah and reigns forever as the risen Lord. The risen Lord is the King and the Lion of the tribe of Judah. Matt 1, Luke 1:26-27, Revelation 5:4-5.

That is, the blessing of the earthly father is two-fold. The father who is sensitive to the Holy Spirit can discern the destiny that God has for the children he's given him and speak that into existence. This godly and spiritually sensitive father can teach his created children to align with the purposes of God at an early age to avoid undue hardship and failures.

Whatever one is, he has been named already, Ecclesiastes 6:10a. There is also a blessing that is a pronouncement and a prophecy from a father to a child that God honours. Our lives are two-fold, what is known to be, and what is spoken to be.

Another example of receiving the father's blessing is the blessing Jacob received from his father Isaac. The blessing that Isaac pronounced over Jacob established him and gave him the right of inheritance to inherit the blessings and the promises God made to Abraham. That is, the father's voice activates the promised inheritance and the blessing that God has already prepared for His Children. Conversely, the voice of the father being used in a negative sense can pronounce difficulty and hardship over his children, as seen in the life of Esau.

Then his FATHER ISAAC SAID to him, "Come NEAR AND kiss me, my son." So he CAME NEAR AND kissed him. And ISAAC smelled the smell of his GARMENTS AND blessed him AND SAID,

"See, the smell of my son is AS the smell of A field THAT the Lord HAS blessed!
MAY God give you of the dew of HEAVEN AND of the FATNESS of the EARTH AND plenty of GRAIN AND wine.

Let peoples serve you,
AND NATIONS bow down to you.
Be lord over your brothers,
AND MAY your mother's sons bow down to you.
Cursed be everyone who curses you,
AND blessed be everyone who blesses you!"

This blessing followed and was manifested in the life of Jacob and He was seen pointing to His spiritual identity, making reference to and calling on the God of his father when He encountered a challenge with Laban.

Thus I HAVE been in your house twenty YEARS; I served you fourteen YEARS for your two DAUGHTERS, AND six YEARS for your flock, AND you HAVE CHANGED my WAGES ten times. Unless the God of my FATHER, the God of ABRAHAM AND the FEAR of ISAAC, HAD been with me, surely now you would HAVE sent me AWAY EMPTY-HANDED. God HAS SEEN my AFfliction AND the LABOR of my HANDS AND rebuked you LAST night."

Genesis 31:41

The presence of a Godly father who is active in the life of his children, releases the children into all that God has for them without a struggle. That is not only will such a father be providing for the needs of his children, the children will also have an opportunity to observe their father's relationship with God and can make the God of their father, their own God as well.

God is a generational God. His dealings with man are not limited to one generation. He wishes that each generation will proclaim His works, dealings, and promises to the next generation. I believe that sometimes God makes certain promises to us and purposely does not carry it out with the generation that received the promise but fulfils that promise in another generation.

One GENERATION SHALL PRAISE Your works to ANOTHER, And SHALL DECLARe Your mighty ACTS.
Psalm 145: 4

Satan is also a generational thinker. When he enslaves one generation, he intends to repeat and perpetuate his acts on generations after that. He does everything to create an evil identity not just for individuals but desires to create it for an entire family for generations. For example, if he succeeds in keeping a father or mother in alcohol addiction, he wants to repeat that same pattern in the next generation.

This then becomes the identity of the family from generation to generation. For the next generations to be free, there must be a recognition of such demonic enslavement and break the power of it through prayer, and by activating the power of the blood. There are many books on breaking generational curses, and we approach this topic not from the point of enslavement but the point of enforcement of the finished work of Christ on the cross.

Christ HAS redeemed us from the curse of the LAW, HAVING become A curse for us (for it is written, "Cursed is everyone who HANGS on A tree"), THAT the blessing of ABRAHAM might come upon the Gentiles in Christ Jesus, THAT we might receive the promise of the Spirit through FAITH.

Galatians 3:13

The attack that has been launched against you may not only be about you. If it were up to the enemy, he would want to make the pain, setback, divorce, sickness your identity, and replicate it in the life of generations after you. But there is a solution in Christ Jesus.

What the enemy tries to do is to break the chain of a godly spiritual heritage. Thus, there might be a family who's had a rich spiritual heritage and the enemy will create a situation to break that chain of blessing. Hence, you may have one generation that may drift away from God, begin to live ungodly lifestyles and thereby abandoning their spiritual inheritance and swaying from the intended purposes of God for their lives. The enemy takes advantage of that and repays the consequences of the sins of one generation on another if that receiving generation does not rise in repentance and demand their freedom. The fullness of our identity is realized when we align with God.

FINDING OUR SPIRITUAL IDENTITY THROUGH CHRIST

The finished work of Christ has given us a new identity in God. An Identity that surpasses any identity we inherit from our biological fathers. Christ balances the equation for all who come from backgrounds that are less than to be desired and have lost inheritances. A broken and fractured identity produces fear, insecurity, iniquity, immorality, and the like. But Christ Jesus came to redeem all that was lost and to gather all things at the feet of the father. He came to redeem and to restore. So even if you never had an identity or cannot trace your identity because you do not know your biological father or mother or never had a healthy relationship with your earthly father, or you feel like you cannot identify with anyone spiritually, Christ Jesus is your point of reference. And what does the word of God say about your identity?

Jesus SAID to him, "TODAY SALVATION HAS come to this house, BECAUSE this MAN, too, is A SON of ABRAHAM. 10 For the Son of MAN CAME to seek AND to SAVE the lost."
Luke 19:9-10

This story brings joy to my heart anytime I read it. It is the story of the man Zacchaeus the Tax Collector. This man had a bad reputation that became his identity. He was known for corruption and charging more than he should in taxes. Most people did not like him, and he was the type of person many would think could gain the favour with Jesus. Yet Jesus took the time to not only speak to Him but to visit him, restoring his identity and his dignity.

What I love about Jesus is that no sin or sinner intimidates him. It does not matter how notorious a sinner you are; He will still visit you and still sit with you and even eat with you. Jesus was well known and respected in His days by many, and when He stopped to fellowship, visit or speak to an outcast, He was communicating and sending a message to the people that If I accept this person, you ought to accept them as well. In so doing He restored not only their reputation but their identity and dignity as well.

That is the same thing He does for us when we receive Him as Lord and saviour. The Apostle Paul said, if any man is in Christ, He is a new creation, old things are passed away, and behold all things are new.

Therefore, if ANYONE is in Christ, he is A new CREATION; old things HAVE PASSED AWAY; behold, ALL things HAVE become new. Now ALL things are of God, who HAS reconciled us to Himself through Jesus Christ, AND HAS given us the ministry of RECONCILIATION, THAT is, THAT God WAS in Christ reconciling the world to Himself, not [d] imputing their TRESPASSES to them, AND HAS committed to us the word of RECONCILIATION.

2 Corinthians 5:17-19

In the Old Testament, we saw a father, Jacob, imputing the sin of his son Reuben against him, giving him an identity based on his past mistakes. But our father God is not like that. He does not recount our sin against us. Instead, he takes off the identity that our sins, mistakes, sickness, and pain has given to us.

One thing that Jesus was careful to do often when He healed and restored someone, was to say, this is also a child of Abraham.

Now He WAS TEACHING in one of the SYNAGOGUES on the SABBATH. And behold, there WAS A WOMAN who HAD A SPIRIT of infirmity eighteen YEARS, AND WAS bent over AND could in no WAY [D]RAISE herself up. But when Jesus SAW her, He CALLED her to Him AND SAID to her, "WOMAN, you ARe loosed from your infirmity." And He LAID His HANDS on her, AND IMMEDIATELY she WAS MADE STRAIGHT, AND glorified God.

But the ruler of the SYNAGOGUE ANSWERed with INDIGNATION, BECAUSE Jesus HAD HEALED on the SABBATH; AND he SAID to the crowd, "There ARe six DAYS on which men ought to work; therefore come AND be HEALED on them, AND not on the SABBATH DAY."

The Lord then ANSWERED him AND SAID, [e]"Hypocrite! Does not EACH one of you on the SABBATH loose his ox or donkey from the STALL, AND LEAD it AWAY to WATER it? So ought not this WOMAN, being A DAUGHTER of ABRAHAM, whom SATAN HAS bound—think of it—for eighteen YEARS, be loosed from this bond on the SABBATH?" And when He SAID these things, ALL His ADVERSARIES were put to SHAME; AND ALL the multitude rejoiced for ALL the glorious things THAT were done by Him.

Luke 13:10-17

In this passage, we see Jesus not only healing the woman but

79

also restoring her identity. For 18 years this woman was bent over. I believe most people may have forgotten her name and might have referred to her as the woman who is bent over. The attacks, infirmity, sickness, poverty, divorce are all Satan's way of trying to impose a false identity on us. Like the woman, you may have gone through a painful experience that may have become your identity, that is exactly what the enemy seeks to do in your life. He does everything in the believer's life to attack their identity in Christ and cause us to doubt our standing in Christ and doubt the love of God.

But be steadfast in the identity God has given you. What is the identity of the New man (the new creation realities)?

If ANY MAN be in Christ he is A new CREATION
2 Corinthians 5:17

Coming to Him AS to A living stone, rejected indeed by men, but chosen by God AND precious, you ALSO, AS living stones, ARe being built up A SPIRITUAL house, A holy priesthood, to offer up SPIRITUAL SACRIFICES ACCEPTABLE to God through Jesus Christ. Therefore it is ALSO CONTAINED in the Scripture,

"Behold, I LAY in Zion
A chief cornerstone, elect, precious,
And he who believes on Him will by no MEANS be put to SHAME." Therefore, to you who believe, He is precious; but to those who [b] ARe disobedient,
"The stone which the builders rejected HAS become the chief cornerstone," AND "A stone of stumbling

And A rock of offense. "They stumble, being disobedient to the word, to which they ALSO were APPOINTED.

But you ARe A chosen GENERATION, A rOYAL priesthood, A holy NATION, His own SPECIAL people, THAT you MAY prOCLAIM the PRAISES of Him who CALLED you out of DARKNESS into His MARVELLOUS light; who once were not A people but ARe now the people of God, who HAD not OBTAINED mercy but now HAVE OBTAINED mercy.

1 Peter 2:4-9

Let's examine what God says about us in this scripture. We are:

- Living stones
- Being built up as a spiritual house (we are a work in progress)
- Called to offer up spiritual sacrifices to God (called to worship God)
- We will never be put to shame (we end in victory no matter the challenge)
- We are a chosen generation
- A Royal Priesthood
- A holy nation
- His own special people
- We are proclaimers of His praise
- We have been called out of darkness (we are a people of light)
- We have obtained mercy

WHERE IS OUR POSITION?

Blessed be the God AND FATHER of our Lord Jesus Christ,

who HAS blessed us with every SPIRITUAL blessing in the HEAVENLY PLACES in Christ, just AS He chose us in Him before the FOUNDATION of the world, THAT we should be holy AND without BLAME before Him in love, HAVING predestined us to ADOPTION AS SONS by Jesus Christ to Himself, ACCORding to the good PLEASURe of His will, to the PRAISE of the glory of His GRACE, by which He [A] MADE us ACCEPTED in the Beloved.

In Him we HAVE redemption through His blood, the forgiveness of sins, ACCORDING to the riches of His GRACE which He MADE to ABOUND TOWARD us in ALL wisdom AND [b]prudence, HAVING MADE known to us the mystery of His will, ACCORDING to His good PLEASURE which He purposed in Himself, THAT in the DISPENSATION of the fullness of the times He might GATHER together in one ALL things in Christ, [c]both which are in HEAVEN AND which are on EARTH—IN Him. In Him ALSO we HAVE OBTAINED AN INHERITANCE, being predestined ACCORDING to the purpose of Him who works ALL things ACCORDING to the counsel of His will, THAT we who first trusted in Christ should be to the PRAISE of His glory.

In Him you ALSO trusted, AFTER you HEARD the word of truth, the gospel of your SALVATION; in whom ALSO, HAVING believed, you were SEALED with the Holy Spirit of promise, who[d] is the [e] GUARANTEE of our INHERITANCE until the redemption of the PURCHASED possession, to the PRAISE of His glory.

Ephesians 1:3-14

- We have been blessed with every spiritual blessing
- He chose us Himself before the foundations of the world
- We are called to live holy and be blameless before Him in love
- We have been adopted through His son Jesus
- We have been accepted in the beloved
- We have redemption and forgiveness of sins
- We know the will of God
- We have an inheritance
- We are the praise of His glory

If then you were RAISED with Christ, seek those things which are ABOVE, where Christ is, sitting AT the right HAND of God. Set your mind on things ABOVE, not on things on the EARTH. For you died, AND your life is hidden with Christ in God. When Christ who is our life APPEARS, then you ALSO will APPEAR with Him in glory.

Colossians 3: 1-4

- We were raised with Christ
- We ought to seek the things which are above
- Set our minds on things above
- Our lives are hidden with Christ in God
- We will appear with God in glory

For God so loved the world THAT He GAVE His only begotten Son, THAT whoever believes in Him should not perish but HAVE EVERLASTING life. For God did not send His Son into the world to condemn the world, but THAT the world through Him might be SAVED.

John 3:16-17

- God loves the world
- God gave his only son
- Whoever believes in God will have everlasting life
- God did not send his Son to condemn the world but to save the world

Having then examined these scriptures, what shall we say is the identity of the believer?

The believer is the beloved child of God who is a precious stone, seated and hidden in Christ, justified and being built up into a spiritual house. This is our identity. Our identity does not include fear, torment, and rejection.

IDENTITY CRUSHERS

Our primary identity comes from our relationship with God. Now there are three main things the enemy tries to use to crush us. These are deception, fear, and sin. Deception is the first weapon that Satan deployed against mankind. His sole purpose with deception is to deceive men from believing what God has said to us about us and has called us to do. If Satan can deceive you from believing the truth of the word of God then he can get you to disobey God and when he gets you to disobey God that creates fear in you because the absence of the presence of God with us or the perceived absence of the presence of God with us creates in us a certain level of fear and insecurity. But when we are fully aware of the word of God and we believe it we are full of faith and will be full of confidence. We are also able to function to the level that God has called us to, therefore the enemy uses this vicious cycle of deception to create fear in us. Fear creates insecurity in us, insecurity causes us to doubt God, and because we do not believe in God, we sin against God by disobeying His word and when we disobey the word of God and walk away from Him, we lose our identity which is the confidence that we have in God.

There is a confidence we have that when we ask God for help, He will provide; that when we pray to God, He will answer. We have an inheritance in God and that inheritance is laid up for us so the enemy deceives us and the purpose of his deception is for us to abandon everything that God has for us and go into the world, and to believe that the enemy has something better for us. Satan tells us lies that make us lose our place in God, lose our identity in God, and abandon the purposes of God for our lives and destiny.

This is the same thing that he did in the garden of Eden, his deception caused man to lose his place with God and abandon his God-given destiny. Man lost the presence of God through deception and sin. But God calls us to our identity in Him, which is that of Sonship. We are accepted in the beloved.

It doesn't matter what we have done, or what has been done to us, or how broken we are. God still calls us His own. We have been chosen, redeemed, loved, and seated with Christ and we are created in Christ Jesus for greater works, our identity is for greater works. It is imperative that we have an understanding of these identity crashers so that when we go through challenges, we will not let that overwhelm us but rather we will see what   is behind the challenges and what the purpose of the enemy is behind the challenges that we face. The pain of rejection and disappointment and all the evil things that come against us is orchestrated by Satan to accomplish one thing and that is to take us away from the presence of God and cause us to reject God. No matter what you are facing now, know that you are not alone, that God is with you and that God is for you, and that God is fighting for you and there is nothing that can change His mind about you because He has loved you.

He always loves you and will continue to love you and right now His arms are open for you to come and receive that healing. Come to him, for it is when you come to Him that your identity is healed and restored and you are made whole. He is our comforter.

DESTINY (GIFTS, TALENT, SCOPE OF INFLUENCE)
When we have a proper, healthy image of ourselves, and God, we can identify and walk in the fullness of our destiny. What is our destiny?
Our destiny is our part in God's agenda for the nations.

For we ARe God's HANDIWORK, crEATED in Christ Jesus to do good works, which God prEPARed in ADVANCE for us to do.

Ephesians 2:10

God's initial plan for man is for man to have dominion over the earth and to multiply in all aspects of life. God believes in multiplication and fruitfulness.

And God blessed them, AND God SAID unto them, Be
fruitful, AND multiply, AND replenish the EARTH, AND
subdue it: AND HAVE dominion over the fish of the SEA,
AND over the fowl of the AIR, AND over every living thing
THAT moveth upon the EARTH.

Genesis 1:28

Yet after the fall, the believer was given a two-fold mandate;
that is to accomplish God's agenda as outlined in Genesis
1:28 and the great commission in Matthew 28:16-20.

Then Jesus CAME to them AND SAID, "All AUTHORITY in
HEAVEN AND on EARTH HAS been given to me. Therefore go
AND MAKE disciples of ALL NATIONS, BAPTIZING them in
the NAME of the FATHER AND of the Son AND of the Holy
Spirit, AND TEACHING them to obey everything I HAVE
COMMANDED you. And surely I AM with you ALWAYS, to
the very end of the AGE."

Matthew 28:16-20

Since the fall of man, God's primary goal has been to restore
man to Himself, as written in first John, the son of God was
made manifest that He might destroy the works of the devil.
The Apostle Paul also said God is reconciling man to himself
not counting man's sin against him but that through Jesus
Christ man may be restored to God.

For this reason, God has given every believer the ministry of
reconciliation, now this ministry of reconciliation is worked
out differently in every believer's life through our gifts, talents,
and everything we do. All that we are and everything we do

must all culminate into fulfilling the purposes of God. Thus, we must come to a place of wholeness so we can identify our purpose and fully thrust ourselves into fulfilling it. It is impossible for us to function fully in the purposes for which God has called us to without having an understanding of who we are, who's we are, and what we are here to do.

When we have a fractured opinion of God, that is when we see God as so far away and not being near us or when we see God through the lenses of our brokenness and earthly disappointments, we have great difficulty opening up to having intimacy and complete alignment with him. God is always seeking to have a deeper and more intimate relationship with us. When couples have a friendship and an intimate relationship with each other, they operate with greater understanding, respect, and a shared vision. In the same vein, when God has complete access to our hearts, He is able to influence our perception, thoughts, and mindset of His Glory. It's about who has possession of us and whose purpose we align with.

When we have a healthy understanding of who God is, His ways, and His character, we can be an expression of His love and goodness towards others. Our relationship with God and the depth of our intimacy with him directly affect our impact and effectiveness. The second thing for us to be able to work fully in our purpose is having a healthy opinion and a healthy understanding of who we are in Christ and we have explored that in the previous passages. But who we are in Christ is that we are chosen, redeemed, set apart, loved, and equipped for good works? Yes, we may have made mistakes, we may have suffered all manner of abuse, yet the father sees us as His own precious people and is willing to heal, deliver, and restore us to wholeness. Wholeness is a possibility we can achieve.

Now there are two forces at work on earth or there are two kingdoms from which we can operate. That is the Kingdom of God and the Kingdom of darkness and each Kingdom is looking for people to work out its agenda. So just as God pours out His Spirit upon His people to do His work, so does the enemy take possession of people to do His bidding.

Satan does all he can to keep his captives forever bound. When he takes possession of a person, he does everything to keep them in the world of sin. He will give them everything, the pleasures of life, the lust of the flesh, and the pride of life. He would give them all to keep them bound. Because he cannot take possession of the believer, he entices us with sin, creates situations to distract us and inhibit our capacity for greatness. Such distractions can be painful contentions, relational trauma, opposition, fear, etc. He is a wicked foe and will deploy anything he can use to distract and destroy.

Satan's weapons and strategies can be categorized into two, pleasure and affliction. He either uses pleasure to entice and distract or uses afflictions to delay and derail. When he is not able to entice us with sin, he comes against us with a deep affliction, that which can cause us to doubt God and even to abandon the faith we profess. But like the Apostle Paul, we must say in all our afflictions that neither death, nor height, nor sickness nor evil, shall be able to separate us from the love of God.

Therefore, know that the affliction that you may be going through, although it may seem like it's all about you, like you're all alone in this battle, know that the battle is not truly about you but it's about God and His plans and purposes for your life. Anytime Satan attacks you, His main aim is to attack the purposes of God in your life. We can also safely say the battle is not ours, but the Lord's and He will fight it. Having this knowledge causes us to have confidence in God that no matter the pain that we're going through now that no matter the hurt that we experiencing, that no matter the fears that are within and without, God is able to deliver and heal us.

Therefore, we do not despair but will look up to Him, the God of all comfort, who comforts us even in our deepest affliction. Whether it be a divorce, financial difficulty, sickness, or any form of affliction, know that your life, everything about you is all for His glory.

But He WAS wounded for our TRANSGRESSIONS, He WAS bruised for our iniquities; The CHASTISEMENT for our PEACE WAS upon Him, And by His stripes[we are HEALED.
Isaiah 53:5

FINDING OUR COMMUNITY AND TRIBE
The relationship between finding an identity and finding our community is one that is very intertwined. Your identity represents who you are, your true nature as God intended you to be. Knowing and accepting our God-given identity

helps us locate the right tribe and community that will bring out the best of God in us. The opposite is true as well, being in the right tribe can equally help you find your true identity.

Now, what do I mean about community and tribe? There is a notion that no man is an island by himself. As human beings, we are created for relationships; we are created to love and to be loved and to form mutually edifying relationships that help us to thrive. The primary reason for God creating man was to
have a relationship with man. Therefore, the creator put a system in man that creates a need to be connected with others. With this need comes the need to be accepted, loved, respected, and valued.

According to Maslow's hierarchy of needs, there are 7 basic needs for every human being. Maslow believes that man functions at his best when these needs are met.

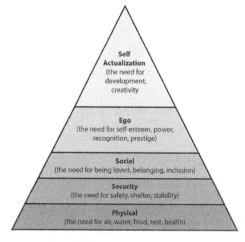

(Psychology TODAY Online)

The two early stages in accordance with Maslow's hierarchy are the physical needs and the safety of a person. Once these are assured, the person moves on to what I call identity formation. That is the social -need to be loved, a place to belong, and the need to be included. The tribe of a person is not necessarily the ethnic group they belong to or their nationality but the group or environment where they feel loved, accepted, and included.

That is, when one finds a group of people who makes them feel loved, accepted, and included in spite of the person's weakness and challenges, they are able to be their true self, knowing that they are accepted for who they are.

Acceptance has a way of bringing out the best in people. It is interesting to note that before Jesus began His Earthly ministry, the Father so lavished His love on Him making a public announcement of who He is and how He (God) sees Him at His baptism.

And when Jesus WAS BAPTIZED, IMMEDIATELY he went up from the WATER, AND behold, the HEAVENS were opened to him, [c] AND he SAW the Spirit of God descending like A dove AND coming to rest on him; 17 AND behold, A voice from HEAVEN SAID, "This is my beloved Son, [d] with whom I AM well PLEASED."

Matthew 3:16-17

God did the same to everyone who runs to Him and accepts Jesus as their Lord and Saviour. The Spirit of God mentioned in the above scripture is the same Holy Spirit who comes to dwell in the believer when the believer accepts Jesus as their saviour. It is as if God is saying, "because you have believed in my Son, I also accept you and to prove that, I will send my spirit, the same Holy Spirit who came to land on my son as a sign of my approval, I will send Him to dwell in you". This time, Emmanuel is not only with us but in us.

Such knowledge of the Father's acceptance of us and the indwelling of His Spirit should serve as acceptance and affirmation that we are loved and accepted by the Lord.

Just AS He chose us in Him before the FOUNDATION of the world, THAT we should be holy AND without BLAME before Him in love, HAVING predestined us to ADOPTION AS SONS by Jesus Christ to Himself, ACCORDING to the good PLEASURE of His will, to the PRAISE of the glory of His GRACE, by which He [A]MADE us ACCEPTED in the Beloved.

Ephesians 1:4-7

What Maslow calls the "Ego" level on His hierarchy of needs is what I call for the believer coming to a place of fulfilment. A place where you have found your place in life and can now work towards producing fruits from the gifts, talents, and opportunities that God has implanted in you.

The next level is what Maslow calls self-actualization, this for the believer is the point of legacy. This is where an individual begins to work on leaving a legacy. They have obtained mastery in every field they operate and at this point, they begin to invest in others. Titus 2 gives examples of this by

93

admonishing the "older women" to teach and guide the younger women.

The older women likewise, THAT they be reverent in BEHAVIOUR, not SLANDERERS, not given to much wine, TEACHERS of good things— THAT they ADMONISH the young women to love their HUSBANDS, to love their children, to be discreet, CHASTE, HOMEMAKERS, good, obedient to their own HUSBANDS, THAT the word of God MAY not be BLASPHEMED.

Titus 2:3-5

We thrive when we are in the right communities and have the right support system. Our community is the people group that God has designed to be in our lives and to help us to achieve the goals and visions God has placed in us.

Community is so important that when a person is found in the wrong community it can stifle their growth and hinder their destiny.

Do not be misled: "BAD COMPANY corrupts good CHARACTER." 1 CORINTHIANS 15:33 yet Proverbs 11:14 SAYS *Where there is no counsel, the people FALL; But in the multitude of counsellors there is SAFETY.*

I have experienced the healing power of a community in many situations. There are times where I experienced grief and great difficulty and it took the presence of others, the presence of loved ones and family, and the church community to speak the words of grace and healing into my soul.

94

When I went through my divorce, I had to rely on the strength of my community to help me to heal. But for many people, although community can be a source of healing, wholeness, love, and comfort, the community can also be the cause of pain, rejection, and deep hurt. Communities can go wrong and toxic, causing pain in the hearts of people. Personally, although I have experienced the love and the comfort of community. I have also had seasons where I have been wounded and broken by the wrong community.

The Lord can use people in our lives, and he can send people our way through whom He can bless us. When the Lord wants to speak to us, He can use people we know and people we do not know. In the same token, when the enemy wants to hurt us deeply, he can use people around us or can send people our way who can cause a lot of damage to us. This happened many times in the Bible and still happens every day.

When the enemy wants to wreck a marriage, he sends situations and people to do his work.

The pain of a toxic community can feel as though God has rejected you and God is against you especially if that community is a church community. Therefore it is important to have an understanding and a knowing of the importance of choosing the right community and better still praying to the Lord that He will lead us into the right communities; the right tribe that will help us be all that God wants us to be.

Now finding the right tribe does not mean that there will

not be conflict, but for us believers, the Bible admonishes us to walk with each other in love, in wisdom, and in honour. Thus, even in the right community, we have to have healthy communication and deal with challenges as they arise in a respectful, godly, an honourable manner to ensure we protect each other's heart, dignity, and create a safe place where we can all call home and a safe community. We must desist from dealing with each other out of the flesh and show kindness, and godliness, bearing all the fruits of the spirit as we relate with one another.

WHAT MAKES A COMMUNITY A HEALTHY COMMUNITY?

A healthy community is one that is centred on respect, love, honour, sacrifice, and service. It is a community the fosters great communication and encourages its members to strive for the best. The community that is right for you will immediately accept you and help you identify the gifts and callings of God in you. This community gives you a voice and creates opportunities for you to manifest in the area of your calling.

In the right community, you will be at liberty to excel and to be all that God has called you to be without fear and without shrinking to please another. The focus of the right community is the development and growth of its people, collective and individual growth. On the contrary, the wrong community may kill your vision and derail your sense of purpose.

Not every community is right for you. While we are advised

to seek the company of others, we must also be discerning about the kind of company we seek. To identify the right community for you, it is essential to have an understanding of who you are as a person and know your purpose. Now let us consider what happens in a toxic and unhealthy community.

For you, brethren, HAVE been CALLED to liberty; only do not use liberty AS AN opportunity for the flesh, but through love serve one ANOTHER. For ALL the LAW is fulfilled in one word, even in this: "You SHALL love your neighbour AS yourself." 15 But if you bite AND devour one ANOTHER, BEWARE lest you be consumed by one ANOTHER!

Galatians 5: 13-15

Now the works of the flesh are evident, which are: [A] ADULTERY, [B]FORNICATION, UNCLEANNESS, lewdness, IDOLATRY, sorcery, HATRED, contentions, JEALOUSIES, outbursts of WRATH, selfish AMBITIONS, dissensions, heresies, envy, [c]murders, drunkenness, revelries, AND the like; of which I tell you BEFOREHAND, just AS I ALSO told you in time PAST, THAT those who PRACTICE such things will not inherit the kingdom of God.

Galatians 5: 13-15

In these verses, the Apostle Paul gives examples of what we must do to avoid creating toxic communities and what we must do to maintain healthy ones. Whenever the natural flesh is given a free flow, it creates environments that wound others and create division.

Thus, if we're in a community and we exhibit the weaknesses of the flesh such as anger, jealousy, malice, bitterness, unfaithfulness, we end up hurting others and giving the enemy the place to operate. Ask yourself, are you in such a community? Were you a contributor to the challenges of the community or were you at the receiving end, or were you a peacemaker?

When we encounter times and seasons when we experience hurt from a community such as church family, a social group, or any other, we must not be hasty to leave the group. Reconciliation should be our priority. A healthy and honest conversation can bring so much healing and understanding in a grievous situation. However, if a community is constantly contentious, offers no opportunity for growth yet constantly depletes your peace and the grace of God on your life, it is prudent to seek the counsel of God as to whether your season with that community has come to an end, or He's creating an opportunity for the community to grow strong through its challenges.

Communities and tribes are a gift of God. He places us in groups with people who share the same spiritual DNA with us so we can encourage each other to do greater works. Allow God to help you locate the right community and tribe that will bring out the best in you.

CHAPTER SIX

TESTIMONIES OF GRIEF, HEALING AND RESTORATION

The story of Pastor Robert is quite a remarkable story of love, joy, grief, and restoration. Pastor Robert married at the age of 26 to the love of his life, lady Judith. The couple met during their time in university at one of the campus student fellowship sessions. These two friends grew fond of each other and got married right after school. The campus fellowship they were a part of later grew and became a notable ministry at which they both served as Pastors.

The couple was blessed with three boys, had a happy home and a successful ministry. 15 years into their marriage lady Judith suddenly died of a heart attack. What a shocking, heart-breaking challenge for Pastor Robert and his family.

What is he going to do without the love of his life? How was he going to raise three boys all under 15? What was life in ministry and at home going to be like without the presence of his wife? God, what was going to become of his boys without their mother? The grief was boundless; fear, anxiety, and questions limitless. How could God be so good yet take my wife so suddenly? I know all things work together for good but how? How can this possibly work together for good? Can anything good come from this situation? Doubtless, these were questions in his mind.

Pastor Robert spent months and years mourning the love of his life while raising their boys alone. The seasons were tough, the nights were long and the questions many. How would God turn this around?

Two years after the death of his wife, Pastor Robert was encouraged to remarry. A decision and a step that was hard to take. Yet the faithfulness of God was abounding in this situation. Two years after the passing of his wife, Pastor Robert remarried and was blessed with a beautiful baby girl a year later.

In the midst of the pain, their heart seemed impossible to heal. How could this be, why would God take away someone so dear to the family, and could healing be possible? Yet the God of all comfort who knows how to comfort the broken-hearted gave Pastor Robert and his children a new start, a new heartbeat in the form of a new mother, wife, a daughter, and a baby sister they had all longed for.

Oh how Pastor Robert loves his little angel Beryl. Beryl is a breath of fresh air to the family. Not only to him but to his boys as well. Finally, a baby sister they could all adore. Beholding the sight of how these brothers adore their baby sister, is a sight that brings tears to eyes and praise to heart to the God who gives beauty for ashes.

In this season of the 2020 pandemic, there are many hearts that have been wounded, broken, and hurt due to the loss of a loved one, their employment, or maybe compromised health. You may have lost someone so precious to you and may be experiencing a heart-wrenching pain while thinking to yourself, will I ever be whole again? Will I ever love again, will my heart heal?

The answer is yes, God sees your heart and understands your pain. He will heal, He will restore and make you whole again. You will smile again. It may not seem like it at this moment, but God can heal.

A FATHER RESTORED

Eleanor's relationship with her father was an interesting one. She loved her father dearly, but her Daddy's choices affected her and her entire family and left them severely broken. Eleanor's parents travelled to Australia leaving her with my father's family when she was 4 years old, her older sister was 6years and her brother was about 3 months old.

The family reunited 10years later when they travelled to Australia at the age of 14. As children, they came with great expectations for the family and their beloved parents whom they had dearly missed; and could not wait to be reunited with them. To their amazement, their father did not seem very thrilled about their coming as it required a change in his lifestyle which he was not ready to accommodate. The story was that her parents had several challenges in their marriage, and this affected the atmosphere in the home. There was constant contention and fear, not knowing when the next argument would be starting. Her father stayed out most of the time and as he would come home from work, change and head out again to hang out with his friends and this was an everyday occurrence. Making adjustments in his lifestyle to accommodate his family was a bitter pill to swallow.

The family life was not something that came easy for him. The concept of being a committed family man was tricky for him as the pull from his friends was much stronger on him than the commitment to his family.

About 6 years after the family arrived in Australia, Eleanor's father decided to move back to his native country in the Caribbean and resettle there, leaving the 3 of his children and the newest addition to their family, their lovely little brother who was under 6 months old to their mother to take care off. This left the family in extreme poverty as the children were all in school and their mother was limited to specific jobs due to certain conditions.

The summer before Eleanor went off to University, she had two jobs, one in a country club which really fueled her desire to succeed in life, and the other being a cleaning job at an old cheese factory. Working at the Country Club exposed Eleanor to a life beyond the one she knew. She saw the lifestyle of the rich and affluent, and this opened a realm of possibilities for her, a future she will earnestly pursue. She came to an understanding that not everyone is struggling, and life did not have to be like she had always known it to be.

Eleanor handed over her cleaning job to her mother when

she went off to school to help supplement her income. When she returned home to attend a University that would allow her to commute to school, she took over the cleaning job which she had handed over to her mother before going off to school. This time around, the money was not going to her but went straight to mum for rent payment.

Sadly, the family later found out that their father was not coming back as he had started a new life in the Caribbean. This left the family in a deep sea of bitterness and resentment, as their hearts were broken, and they felt a sense of abandonment.

About 4 years later, Eleanor's father returned to Australia in an attempt to reunite with his family which he abandoned but this time around, his wife had had enough and was done with him and the marriage. He lived in a separate place and unfortunately got attacked with a stroke. This was one of the most challenging times for Eleanor, seeing her father in that condition and thinking about all the challenges they went through as a family due to his absence was heart-breaking. There were a lot of rumours going in the community about their family and there were times that Eleanor would feel ashamed to even to go out amongst the people who knew the challenges her family was experiencing. She felt stigmatized. In the midst of all the shame and pain Eleanor and her family were experiencing, she held on to her faith and the belief that God, the God that she served had a better plan for her life and that of her family and she was determined to hold on to that faith and press until she obtained the promises God had for her and her family. This meant that she had to be there for her father who had a stroke and support him financially. He later decided to go back to the Caribbean and reside there permanently. The family was very cross with him and for a while, Eleanor was the only one who had any contact with him. This was not because she was the good one, but only because she felt an obligation as a Christian to be the one to stand in the gap for her family until God brought healing and restoration. There were many years of pain, anger, and bitterness but in time, God reunited the family in communication and her other sibling also took on some of the financial responsibility of taking care of their father.

The lesson here is that, if God wants to use you to bring healing and restoration to your family, you may have to go through seasons where you bear the burden of the family alone. Bearing the burden of the family could mean being the spiritual intercessor, the advisor, the peacemaker, and the one providing financial support to your family or others who are in need. You will have to rise to the occasion and hold the family in prayer and sometimes providing financially until God completes His work in the heart of the other members of the family as it was in Eleanor's case. It is not easy to take on such a burden, but God is faithful. Taking on the role of a peacemaker means that sometimes you will have to face the wrath of family members who may not be too thrilled and will not understand why you would want to be there for someone who may have caused you and your family tremendous pain. For Eleanor, this was a long and painful journey, and It might be a long and painful journey for you as well but always know that you are never alone in the fight for your family. God is with you to see His work accomplished in your family; you are just a vessel through whom He works. For Eleanor, to see her family healed, father saved, and to hear her call her Pastor makes every bit of her journey to restoration worthwhile.

You are not alone in this fight for your family, like Moses, you are just a vessel that God is using to bring deliverance and wholeness to your family; work with Him. Looking at Eleanor's story, we can clearly deduce that her family was in real bondage. Often, we underestimate the power of sin but there is no sin greater than the power of God to heal and to restore.

Sin has lost its power because of the death and resurrection of Christ. But man, when man chooses sin over righteousness, especially when that person is the head of the family, the power of sin dominates their lives, and their family suffers the consequences of their sin. The Bible says that the children of the righteous are blessed after him, but God punishes the iniquity of the ungodly even on the children. Yet God, being merciful desires to bring healing and restoration to families and He needs individuals within families to rise and be the channels of healing and restoration. Friend, serving the Lord has great benefits and when you get the chance to be a channel of healing and restoration to your family and others, do not reject it. Ask God for the grace to rise up and be the "saviour" of your family.

For years Eleanor felt there was something missing in her life; like she was missing the love, affection, and blessings of a father. Although she had contact with her dad, it was always a one-sided relationship where his contact with her was on a need basis. He would only reach out to her when he had a need, there was nothing about him showing a sense of care or affection towards her and her siblings. There was never a time where he would call just to check on her or to see how she and the family were doing. Sometimes, when he would call and ask for money and her response would be a no or wait, he would hang up in frustration without even giving her the chance to finish her sentence. Eleanor lived feeling like an orphan, always looking for that father figure to connect with. This made her quite vulnerable as she would attach herself to "father" figures.

Eleanor testifies there were true father figures whom God brought into her life who genuinely and sincerely cared for her. She credits her church Pastors and leadership for providing support, love, and leadership in times when she needed such.

Unfortunately for Eleanor, she experienced the painful journey of a divorce 4 years after her marriage. Even through her divorce, the concept of a father's comfort and support was not something received from her father. Through all these bitter experiences, she was ever sure of the love and the comfort of God. Eleanor knew and had the conviction that though her earthly father had never fully played his role as a father, God, her heavenly father loved, accepted, and supported her, and that assurance of the presence and provision of God, brought her through her most difficult trials.

Eleanor had experienced painful experiences all her life but going through a divorce was not something she was prepared for. For years she had lived her life trusting that God would give her rest in her matrimonial home and for her, her marriage was going to be the source of her comfort, healing, and wholeness. She had forgotten that vain is the help of man and the one who places great expectations on the arm of flesh is bound to be sorely disappointed. The divorce broke Eleanor to the point that she felt she needed to go away to see the Lord and to find wholeness in the presence of God.

Eleanor journeyed away from the shores of Australia to Europe to a Bible College where she encountered God and found healing and wholeness as she had never experienced before. The Lord really did a deep internal and emotional work on her, bringing up age-old emotional wounds she had suffered even from childhood, through broken relationships, and even though the divorce and beyond. Eleanor is naturally known to be of a sweet personality, likable, and always laughing, but these old and new wounds really tried to bury the sweet, outgoing personality that God gave her.

She developed a fit of latent anger that would surface at home and with minimal triggers. After her divorce, she was filled with so much rage that she would have an outburst with the slightest provocation. Her poor family had to put up with her outbursts and fits of rage. Like Eleanor, I experience similar occurrences when I went through my divorce. I can relate to so much of Eleanor's challenges because as a young lady, I went through my own challenges with my family and also recently went through a divorce. I was so broken and hurt by my divorce because it was never something that I wanted for myself and I fought to resist the divorce but my husband was determined to get the divorce he badly wanted. Like Eleanor, I relied on the support of my family and there was one incident that made me realize that I needed to seek the Lord for healing.

I do not recall exactly what I was angry about but I had some heated exchanges with my brother and my mother and after I settled in my emotions, my brother came to me and said, "Akos, you can't go on like this, you really need to seek help with this anger". That was a turning point for me. I knew I was not an angry person by nature and if I allowed this divorce, it would change who I am for the worse, it would be a double loss. That is, to lose your marriage and your personality along with it. This started my journey of seeking the Lord for healing and wholeness and the Lord started working on my heart in my times of intimacy with Him. He directed me to enroll in the Bible College of Wales, in Swansea, and this was a journey worth taking.

Like Eleanor, I had challenges with my father, not because I was a naughty child, on the contrary, I was a very devoted child and the story of Eleonor made it into this book because in so many ways it seems we both shared very similar experiences that I did not have to tell my story but in telling her story, I welcome my readers to a glimpse of some of my personal experiences.

While I had given up on ever having a good relationship with my father, the Lord was at work. Unbeknownst to me, my Aunt who introduced me to the Lord, who is also a caretaker for my father had been witnessing to him and had been taking him to church. While I was at the Bible College, I got in contact with my father after almost a year of not speaking with him. We reconnected and on the day of my graduation, I called him and asked him to pray for me after the leaders from the college had prayed for us. I felt I needed the blessing of my father even after the commissioning prayer. He agreed and prayed for me. The commissioning prayer from the leaders of the Bible College broke the orphan spirit in me and when my father prayed for me and blessed me, I felt this sense of wholeness come upon me, like the well of restoration swelling over my soul and my life changed for the better since then. I can say, I am a whole person now, healed, and restored. All the hurts and the wounds from the past are healed, I have received the ability to truly forgive with the help of the Holy Spirit. I'm not holding bitterness and anger against anyone and all I want to do is to love people and show them the love of God.

Sincerely loving those who have hurt you is not humanly possible, but with the help of the Holy Spirit, He makes all things possible. There is healing in God and that healing starts with forgiveness when you choose forgiveness over anger.

Like me, Eleanor testifies that she forgave her father and reconnected with him, and through their connection, God brought healing to her entire family and as the time she told me her store, the family has begun a journey of healing and restoration. My prayer for Eleanor is that God who began a good work in her and her family will perfect His work in them as He unites them in love.

In His time, He brings all things together in perfect unity. If you are believing God for the restoration and healing of your family, trust God that He can bring it to pass. Open your heart, be obedient to his leading and watch Him restore everything the enemy destroyed.

God loves us so dearly and is always looking to bless and restore us. Pastor Jenetzen Franklin said, "What God cannot restore, He will replace". You may have a similar story with a father, mother, or a loved one but may not be able to reconcile with them as they may not be physically alive. God is still able to heal you and bring relationships in your life that will eradicate every pain and give you the family life you have always dreamed off. Never underestimate what God can do in your life. He is a good God.

He HAS MADE everything BEAUTIFUL in its time. Also He HAS put eternity in their HEARTS, except THAT no one CAN find out the work THAT God does from beginning to end.
Ecclesiastes 3:11

CHAPTER SEVEN

WHOLENESS THROUGH FORGIVENESS

"For if you forgive men their trespasses, your heavenly Father will also forgive you. But if you do not forgive men their trespasses, neither will your Father forgive your trespasses.

Matthew 6:14-15

If there is a topic that I'm so passionate and eager to write about, it is the topic of forgiveness. Father God is equally passionate about forgiveness because He knows the power of it. I believe forgiveness is a paramount key to receiving the favour of God and getting God on your side when you are wronged, and the opposite also holds. What then is forgiveness and why is it so important to God?

The act of forgiveness is choosing not to charge some's offenses against them and letting go of anything they owe you. It is relinquishing your right to hold a grudge or demand vengeance or compensation for what another person may have done to you. Essentially to forgive someone is to say they do not owe you regardless of what they have done against you.

The question is often asked, can we forgive someone who has not repented? Is repentance a necessity for forgiveness?

I believe you can forgive someone who is neither sorry nor has repented from their wrongdoing. This is because forgiveness is not necessarily for the other person but more so about your personal commitment to obey the command of God to forgive. This is exactly what Father God has done for us. Before we even go to him to ask for forgiveness, He has already made it available. Through His death, resurrection, and ascension, Jesus made provision for our forgiveness. That is, He paid the debt to Father God for every sin anyone would ever commit on earth. Thus, He also paid the debt, and the only requirement to receive this forgiveness is to believe that He paid the debt with His blood and be a partaker of Him.

In that same way, I believe it is possible for us to forgive an offender who is not remorseful or repentant. Forgiveness is not necessarily to the benefit of the offender but the choice of the victim or offended to not hold a charge against the offender.

WHY IS FORGIVENESS SO IMPORTANT TO GOD?

The Lord forgives and will forgive anyone for any sin they commit no matter how grievous the sin is. I state again, there is no sin or wrongdoing that intimidates God. Yet there are two types of people that the Lord will not forgive; the person who blasphemes against the Holy Spirit and the one who will not forgive others of their offenses.

"Therefore, I SAY to you, every sin AND BLASPHEMY will be forgiven men, but the BLASPHEMY AGAINST the Spirit will not be forgiven men.

Matthew 12:31

For if you forgive other people when they sin AGAINST you, your HEAVENLY FATHER will ALSO forgive you. 15 But if you do not forgive others their sins, your FATHER will not forgive your sins.

Matthew 6:14-15

Great is the pain of unforgiveness, for the person who refuses to forgive suffers twice. The pain of unforgiveness is twice as much as that of the offense. That is, the consolation of the person hurt or offended is that God will heal, restore, and vindicate them. However, if we refuse to forgive, we shorten the hand of God from reaching us. As loving and as kind as God is, He will not go against His word. Yet He does not aggressively impose His will upon us but gently leads us to accept His will for our lives.

"Therefore, behold, I will ALLURe her, Will bring her into the wilderness. And SPEAK comfort to her.15 I will give her VINEYARds from there. And the VALLEY of Achor AS A door of hope; She SHALL sing there, As in the DAYS of her youth. As in the DAY when she CAME up from the LAND of Egypt."

Hosea 2:14-15

We must understand that God loves people. He loves us even when we are at our worse and He delights in showing mercy towards us. But He can only forgive us when we

113

decide to forgive others. God in His mercy understands that sometimes we need time to come to the place of forgiveness, and He is patient enough to wait on us so He can be to be gracious to us.

Therefore, the Lord will wait, that He may be gracious to you; And therefore, He will be exalted, that He may have mercy on you. For the Lord is a God of justice; Blessed are all those who wait for Him. Isaiah 30:17-19

Secondly, holding on to unforgiveness is holding on to the pain of the act. Releasing the pain and the offender releases the hand of God to move on your behalf.

You may be saying, how can I forgive someone or the people who have hurt me so deeply? I can understand your pain. I may not have experienced the same magnitude or intensity of pain as you, but I have experienced various levels of pain and betrayal from employers, family, loved ones, and a spouse. Yet in all these, I have come to understand that there is a God who heals and with his arms wide open, welcomes us into His loving and gracious arms. The first step to achieving the healing we need is through forgiveness. Letting go of the things and the people who hurt us frees us to receive the healing we need from God.

MY JOURNEY INTO FORGIVENESS

While I desist from going into details about events that led to the end of my marriage, I will share the lessons I have learnt from that challenge. If we are going to be successful in our Christian walk, there is a need to listen and to trust the leading of the Holy Spirit. But the path of the just is like the shining [a]sun, that shines ever brighter unto the perfect day. Proverbs 4:18.

The path of the righteous will only shine bright when the righteous learn to walk in tune with the Holy Spirit. The Holy Spirit is a gift from God to the believer for guidance, direction unto righteousness, and victorious living over sin and the enemy. Often many believers walk themselves into trouble and endanger their lives when they do not listen and adhere to the guidance of the Holy Spirit. Do not be disobedient in an effort to be resilient and see things through to the end when the Lord is trying to lead you into safety. When the enemy attacked our marriage and my husband's heart was turned from me and there was serious contention in the home, the Holy Spirit tried to lead me to a place of safety and peace but I insisted on staying in the home to work things out and pray through the challenges until I see victory.

When the enemy grabs hold of the will of a person, you cannot change their will until they decide to yield it over to God or God by his sovereignty and power steps into the situation to bring peace and calmness. However, when in the heat of the storm the Holy Spirit instructs you, obey that specific instruction rather than rely on your general knowledge of what you perceive the Lord will do. I call this situation obedience.

Our marriage was not perfect, but we were getting on and growing stronger by the day, but the enemy attacked suddenly and things changed for the worse with the introduction of the strange woman from my partner's workplace.

The Lord knowing the condition of my husband's heart and the decision he had taken, tried to get me to a place where I would be emotionally safe yet I wanted to remain in the home thinking that my presence and prayer would change his heart but it only got worse. God knew the decision he had taken and what He had said to his family to get their support. I believe God knew it was best for me to take the word of my ex-husband that he was no longer interested in the marriage and there was nothing on my part that I could do to change his mind. My presence in that home convicted him of his wrongdoing which he was not ready to repent off and as such maltreated me in such as manner that would make me leave on my own accord, oh but I had a "stubborn faith", which was really disobedience to God and put myself in harm's way. As a wife filled with faith, I was ready to fight for my marriage, I was determined to stay, pray, and work things out, even though I was going through emotional abuse, neglect, and all manner of humiliation. I have chosen not to recount the details of that horrific emotional, and mental agony I endured within that period.

The truth is, the Lord knew my ex-husband's mind was made up and that He wanted a divorce and there was nothing that anyone would say that would change his mind. On an occasion, we had a counselling session with one of our leaders, the leader spent hours talking to us, trying to help us navigate through our challenges, my ex-husband looked me right in the face and said, "do not think what he has said will change my mind, my mind is made up and no one can change it, I will cut you out of my life for good".

Beloved, God is the judge of all hearts, when you encounter a situation, seek the mind of God, and when He gives you an answer, follow it. Do not assume your own answer out of a situation beyond what God has said to you. You may put yourself through undue hardship when you presume that God will give an answer based on your assumptions, faith works best when you have received a word of assurance of God about His intended outcome. It is on that word that you stand and battle through to see the intended outcome. However, if the Lord gives you a contrary word, take it knowing that He has the best of intentions for you.

Through my disobedience to the Holy Spirit and my stubborn determination to get my desired solution, which was reconciliation, I endured unnecessary hardship when my husband's heart was turned against me. How that must grieve the Father, to see His precious daughter going through difficulty yet not willing to hear and obey His voice and His leading.

While I was praying for the situation to change, God was prompting me to move from that toxic environment. When the rage of Esau was aroused against Jacob, God kept Jacob in Laban's house to keep him from the sword of his brother Esau until such a time came when the anger of Esau was subsided and he could receive his brother in peace. We often want to resolve challenges and conflicts expediently, yet some situations require time for healing and reflection and we must come to terms with the reality that we may not get the outcomes we desire in certain situations as it was in my case; the marriage ended in a divorce. A divorce I dreaded, a divorce I did not want. But I can say God has been more than faithful to me and I have grown and discovered potentials in me that were latent and buried under fear, insecurities, and the need for acceptance. God hates divorce but He certainly knows how to comfort the broken and make all things turn out for our good, this is exactly what he has done for me. The compensation and growth God has brought from within me is beyond me. I am in awe.

The Lord is NEAR to those who HAVE A broken HEART, And SAVES such AS]HAVE A contrite spirit. MANY are the AFFLICTIONS of the righteous, But the Lord delivers him out of them ALL. He GUARDS ALL his bones; Not one of them is broken

Psalm 34:18-20

This is the story of a young man and a young woman whose life the enemy tried to destroy. As a young lady growing up in the church, I never thought that I would be divorced at 32. I had the privilege of having a very intimate relationship with the Lord at a young age and by all accounts, divorce should not have been a part of my story. "Why do I say so? I will elaborate more on this. My ex-husband made some bad choices in the way he handled himself and treated me, but I believe there is goodness in him, as I have experienced the good side of him as well as the bad side of him. My prayer for him is that he will surrender totally to God and allow God to heal him from the weaknesses that led him to make those decisions.

To the married men, I say it is imperative to guard your heart and guard yourself by not entertaining other women in what may seem like an innocent and casual conversation. You may not think much of it but it can develop into something that could cost you dearly. There is a part of you as a married man or woman that must be exclusive to you and your partner, when you open the door of your heart and mind to a person whose aim is to destroy your home, you set yourself up for failure.

The focus of this book is to magnify the work of healing the Lord has done in my heart. It goes without saying that a woman will go through tremendous pain whenever there is an introduction of another woman who turns the heart of her husband away from her, and her tears are met with aggression instead of compassion and willingness to change, and worse, be sent away from her home in a divorce. Such was the ordeal I went through towards the end of my marriage.

WHY WE SHOULD NOT HAVE FAILED
Trust AND obey, for there's no other WAY, To be HAPPY in Jesus, but to trust AND obey.

John H. SAMMIS

The believer's journey is one that requires faith and obedience. If we are going to be believers who experience and have divine escapes from the enemy's attacks, we must be people who are willing to Hear and Obey the voice of the

Lord. I say I should not have failed in my marriage and here is the reason.

I had the privilege of having a conversation with a young lady who had gone through tremendous pain and disappointments but also experienced great redemption from God. For the purpose of anonymity, I will call her, Rosa.

Rosa was a girl who had a very intimate relationship with God at a very young age. For a girl who had the privilege of encountering the Lord at a young age, the outcome of Rosa's story should have been life's should have been different but for her disobedience.

Though Rosa grew up in a non-Christian home, the family knew about God but were not committed to serving and worshipping God. However, she was later introduced to a youth group and through this group Rosa encountered God. She met some young men and women from the youth group who were on fire for God and through her affiliation with these young people, she was introduced to preachers such as Derek Prince, Jentezen Franklin, Peter Tan, Benny Hinn, and many others.

Rosa was giving a book by Pastor Benny Hinn called "Good Morning Holy Spirit "and "God's General" by Robert Lairdon and it changed her life completely.

From then on, Rosa had the desire to seek God intimately and the Holy Spirit was faithful to His word and did not withhold His presence from Rosa. Rosa testifies that she had a deep desire for worship and had a real hunger for the study of the Word. Each morning the Lord would wake her up at exactly 4am to fellowship with Him and study His Word before starting her day. This went on uninterrupted for about 5 years of Rosa's life.

The Lord gave her many revelations into His Word and also gave her many prophetic dreams that were solutions to people's questions and challenges.

She developed a reputation for herself in school as the "Jesus girl". Her church folk knew her as the "spiritual girl", the girl who was on fire for God, and truly her faith was sincere, and she genuinely loved the Lord.

She recounts that one day, a young man who was a friend of hers approached her for a relationship to which she responded, "I need time to pray about it". This weighed heavily on her as she knew she was not ready for a relationship but did not want to hurt this good friend of hers and also questioned what if he was God's choice for her.

On Sunday while on her way to church, Rosa felt a strong urge to say no as she was truly not ready for a relationship. I am off the opinion that the Lord was working on Rosa and wanted to build her into the vessel that He wanted to use, thus, it was not time for Rosa to engage in a relationship.

Rosa recounts that while at the service, there was a guest preacher who gave a word of knowledge as he was speaking, and this came as a confirmation to Rosa not to enter any relationship. Again she heard the Lord in her prayer time specifically telling her not to get involved as it was not the time for her to be in a relationship and that getting into a relationship at that time will lead to series of hurts and disappointments. Yet despite all these warnings, Rosa went ahead and agreed to be in a relationship with the young man and this led to a series of hurts in her life. Rosa did not heed to the voice of God and entered that relationship but three months later, she ended the relationship. Although she felt convicted and ended the relationship three months later, a principle was broken, she had compromised on her obedience to God. Although she did not compromise. On her purity with this person, as they were both strong on maintaining their purity, a principle was broken. Rosa blatantly disobeyed the voice of the Holy Spirit who had blessed her with his awesome presence and fellowship for so many years.

This decision to disobey the Lord, although Rosa indicates was not deliberate but out of fear and peer pressure, lead to many seasons of pain, hurts, and disappointments.

Looking into Rosa's experience and my personal season of disobedience, I have come to understand that many of our challenges in life can be traced to an act of disobedience or sin. The question is, how does one act of disobedience lead to hurt upon hurt?

To my understanding, it is not so much that one act of disobedience but more so what that act does to us and in our hearts. I perceive that a certain depth of protection and affinity with the Holy Spirit was broken off due to her disobedience.

Personally, I experienced a similar occurrence of disobedience as it pertains to a relationship. I came to a crossroad of decisions regarding a particular relationship. The Lord showed me in a dream what the outcome of that relationship would be but in the natural, this seemed very unlikely as the person involved at that point seem like a perfect match for me, and at the point of decision, I did not heed to the warnings of the Lord and experience tremendous pain and disappointment when the relationship came to an end just as the Lord had shown in the dream.

Like Rosa, my disobedience led to hurts upon hurts and truly led me to a season of unwarranted wilderness. I went from an innocent girl with the purest of hearts to a wounded girl seeking love in the wrong people. God's plan was for me to be satisfied with His love until He was ready to release me to the one He had planned for me. His plan for me did not include failed relationships. His plan for me was for a peaceful and loving marriage, but through my disobedience, I forfeited His perfect plan for me by going ahead of Him. Thus, by the time my ex-husband came along, my heart was wounded from past relationships and had insecurities and fears that impacted how I handled any perceived external threats.

Sadly, he came into the marriage with his own brokenness and unresolved issues that led to his attachment to the strange woman at work.

123

ENCOUNTERING MYSELF

When my marriage ended and the reality of a painful divorce set in, I came to God with many questions. The famous question being, God why? Why did you allow this to happen to me? Why am I going through such pain and humiliation? Though had many questions and sometimes accusation towards God, yet I still felt the comfort of God as I encountered His truth.

The Lord reminded me of the many warnings he gave me concerning relationships and how he wanted to establish me in the right relationship at the right time, yet I would not listen to Him. I can emphatically say that any time I entered into relationships that was not in the will of God for me, the Lord would show me in a dream or speak to me concerning the outcome of that relationship in my quiet time; yet somehow I foolishly ignored the promptings of the Lord being confused and thinking I would lose out if this person if turned out to be God-sent and with that mindset went into wrong relationships.

I remember after leaving my first relationship, 2 years later another person friend showed interest in me asked for a relationship me and again I resulted to seek the Lord. This time I fasted and on the third day of the fast, I had a dream. In this dream, I saw that I was in a relationship with this man and somehow, he left me and went for another lady. I was so shocked and in disbelief that I was crying like a baby in the dream and when I woke up from the dream, I had physical tears in my eyes. The dream was so vivid that I saw the face of the girl whom he had left me for and it was not

124

someone we both knew but and about a year later, this man met this girl and the inevitable happened. I took the dream as a warning from the Lord and this time around I said no to this person. Yet in the natural, there was no reason at that time to believe that what I saw in the dream was true.

The man in question was so caring, seemed to genuinely care for me. Shared the same passion I had for God and even urged me to go deeper in the Lord. He was an avid reader and introduced me to many authors and Holy Spirit-filled preachers and was persistent in seeking God. I began to believe he was the will of God for me despite the warning from the dream. After some months of entertaining this person and not saying a definite no, my senses and judgment were so clouded and like a foolish sheep, I walked myself into another relationship that God had warned me against. A year later, the dream I had come to pass just as I had seen it.

While the Lord reminded me of these missteps, He also brought me to a place of understanding as to how the enemy uses our disobedience as a weapon against us. These missteps created in me a fear, mistrust, and unhealed wounds. In these situations, God was not after my relationships but rather needed my obedience to His promptings to keep me from setting myself up for a greater disappointment. One cannot tell what the future holds but the future becomes predictable when you are properly aligned with God, that is, proper alignment with the will and purposes of God brings peace and stability. It is never for the benefit of God that we obey Him but rather it is in our own interest and benefit to obey God, He rewards obedience.

We cannot afford to live in disobedience. Disobedience is costly. Life is not only about prayer and doing everything you think is in line with God, you need to know the voice of God in every situation, what He requires of you as an individual, and follow it, irrespective of what others are doing. My brokenness made me very insecure and I believe it affected my relationships greatly.

From an incredibly young age, I sensed that God had something great for me to do. I believe the Lord was grooming me for His peculiar purpose and the enemy was also working diligently to interrupt and to sabotage the work, and dealings of God in my life. What stood between the enemy and God, was my obedience or disobedience. Your obedience or disobedience to the voice of the Lord determines your success as a Christian. But like me, if you have had the enemy try to sabotage the dealings of the Lord in your life, know that God will not give up on you as He did not give up on me. Even as I write this book, the Lord has opened many great doors for me and given me the ability to do in one year what I could not do in 10 years. The enemy meant to use divorce as a means to sabotage and stop what God is doing in my life, but glory be to God that He has turned it around and is using it for his glory. I can say I am living Romans 8:28 and Genesis 50:20.

And we know THAT ALL things work together for good to those who love God, to those who ARe the CALLED ACCORding to His purpose.

Romans 8:28

But AS for you, you MEANT evil AGAINST me; but God MEANT it for good, in order to bring it ABOUT AS it is this DAY, to SAVE MANY people ALIVE.

Genesis 50:20

What the enemy meant for evil in my life, God has turned it around for good. God's grace is bigger and greater than our mistakes and missed steps, purpose overrides attacks.

I must say, going into a marriage with a wounded heart and unhealed emotions do not mean that the relationship will fail. There've been people who have been through worse situations than I have yet God used a wholesome marriage to heal their hearts and brought wholeness to them through their marriage.

As a couple, we both had unresolved issues but were getting on and we grew stronger and better each day. However, the enemy was swift to take advantage of my absence and use the minor pending issues we had as a catalyst to break the marriage. He completely turned the heart of my husband against me with the introduction of a strange woman. But more importantly, the Lord has brought me through and healed me and the best part is that He has equipped me with the wisdom I need to make better choices in a relationship. What I love about the Lord is that He gives you the truth in love. While going through the healing process, though I was greatly wronged by the actions of my husband. He also showed areas where I missed it as a wife and taught me the wisdom, needed to manage future occurrences should I ever encounter a situation like that in the future.

When you encounter God, He does not leave you the same. He confronts your weaknesses and mistakes and gives you the wisdom and the grace you need to overcome them. The old person, the girl who was angry, insecure, bitter, and heartbroken died and a new girl has emerged. One who is confident in all areas because she has tasted the goodness of the Lord and knows she can trust God with her life. One who has completely forgiven herself for the bad decisions she made and forgiven those whose bad decisions left her broken, one who is obedient and will not decide without hearing and following the voice of the Lord.

One who has risen up in her calling and is making strides for the Kingdom of God. Boy, I wish I had met this girl earlier because I'm loving this girl. The God of all Comfort has comforted and rebuilt a brand new girl out of the old girl, Praise be to His name!

FINDING MERCY, FORGIVENESS, AND WHOLENESS

By 2018, my life was in complete and utter shambles. Divorced at age 32, covered with shame as the divorce came with made- up stories to discredit who I am as a means of covering up and justifying how I was treated. I returned to Canada broken, shamed, jobless, accused, and hopeless; not knowing what was next for my life. The emotional and mental turmoil was unbearable.

But God was ever merciful. In the midst of my shame, pain, hurts, and hopelessness, I cried out to the Lord. He is the one friend that I knew I could count on for truth, mercy, and grace. I confessed my sin of this disobedience and for not allowing Him to do with me what he had intended to do in my life from my youth.

I wept many nights, sometimes calling on God to take vengeance on all who had caused me such great harm. The Lord greatly comforted me and there are some key verses in the Bible that the Holy Spirit gave to comfort me and as a sign of that He will do in my life.

Bless the Lord, O my soul;
And ALL THAT is within me, bless His holy NAME! Bless the Lord, O my soul,
And forget not ALL His benefits:
Who forgives ALL your iniquities, Who HEALS ALL your DISEASES,
Who redeems your life from destruction,
Who crowns you with lovingkindness AND tender mercies,
Who SATISFIES your mouth with good things,

So THAT your youth is renewed like the EAGLE's. The Lord executes righteousness and justice for ALL who are oppressed. He MADE known His WAYS to Moses, His ACTS to the children of ISRAEL.
The Lord is merciful AND GRACIOUS, Slow to ANGER, AND ABOUNDING in mercy. He will not ALWAYS strive with us, Nor will He keep His ANGER forever.
He HAS not DEALT with us ACCORDING to our sins, Nor punished us ACCORDING to our iniquities.

For AS the HEAVENS are high ABOVE the EARTH,
So GREAT is His mercy TOWARD those who FEAR Him; As

FAR AS the EAST is from the west,
So FAR HAS He removed our TRANSGRESSIONS from us. As
A FATHER pities his children,
So the Lord pities those who FEAR Him. For He [A]KNOWS
our FRAME;
He remembers THAT we are dust

He made me understand that what I thought were ashes and the mistakes that I felt had disqualified me from what He wanted to do in my life was the very thing He would use as a platform to accomplish His purpose in my life. See, like Moses, we may feel disqualified because of our mistakes, yes the timing of God may be delayed and we may miss some key people that were part of God's original plan for our lives but as long as we stay close to Him, He knows how to reshuffle the pieces of our puzzle and put us back together to create the art of our lives that He has intended from the beginning.

I once heard a man of God say, David was not God's original choice of a king but rather a replacement for a king who lost his throne but David is considered the greatest king Israel has ever had.

Solomon was a product of a union that God never recognized (the Bible always referred to Bathsheba as Uriah's wife) yet next to his father, and is considered and praised for his unmatched wisdom.

God creates beautiful art out of broken pieces.

While I take full responsibility for my disobedience, the Lord helped me to fully understand what this battle was all about. The interruption was all part of Satan's agenda to derail and stop the work of God in my life. God has an investment in my life, there is an assignment on my life and the enemy has tried all He can to stop me from achieving the purposes of God for my life. His will is for me to carry out the message of His grace to the world, yet the enemy's agenda was to try to stop God's purposes in my life. This is not peculiar to me.

In my life the enemy used relationships, he may have used different situations in your life to sabotage the work of God in you and through you. The important thing to note is that the will of God for us is to escape satanic entrapment, and if by the reason of our disobedience and weakness we are trapped, there is grace for redemption.

It is important to note that the only way I found my healing was through forgiveness. Yes, the enemy had an agenda, and it was executed through the wickedness and the weakness of man. My human heart in my pain would not focus on the grand agenda of the enemy but the human vessels he used. That is, as I recognized my need for forgiveness, I knew that I had to forgive those through whom the enemy used to cause me so much pain. That is, I had to forgive my ex-husband, his family, and the lady involved in the breaking of our marriage. It was a painful process to go through, but the Lord gave me victory. I also had to forgive myself for the pain I allowed into my life.

The only way I could forgive them was to first develop compassion for them. I came to an understanding that God loves people, the good, the bad, the ugly, and all. As much as this situation has caused me pain, I know that it has greatly affected my ex- husband as well. When he looks back at how he treated me and from the background He comes from, growing up in a ministerial home, I know this would cause him pain as I imagine that he was raised to do better than how he treated me.

I began to have compassion for the lady as well because her pain and her jealousy led her to wreck our home because she had experienced the pain of divorce twice and yet did not bring herself before God to be healed and transformed and be made better but rather created an avenue for the enemy to afflict her more and face the consequences of her sin against our home.

When I came to this understanding, I started praying for them, asking God to bring healing to them and bring them to a place of repentance so their sins can be forgiven.

Besides understanding the need to forgive them, I needed a practical way to activate and exercise that forgiveness. That is, my heart needed to be healed, and needed to find hope that this was not the end of me. The Lord reminded me and truly gave me a revelation of REDEMPTION.

Redemption is the focal point of Christianity. Without redemption, there is no Christianity. That is, God's original intent was to have His kind of fellowship with man, and his plans for man to be equipped with dominion was thwarted by the enemy, yet God redeemed man to Himself through

Jesus Christ the second Adam. Another way that I found healing was through worship and fellowship with the Holy Spirit. To me worshipping God and fellowshipping with the Holy Spirit is the key to dealing with issues we cannot see but are in us and causing damage to us.

Whenever we worship God, we exalt His divinity and release our humanity. In worship, His presence is manifested, and we experience the joy and love of his presence. I remember there were times in worship that I would cry my heart out and other times my heart will swell with joy just by being in His presence, it was as if the oil of gladness was poured on me.

You may be reading this book because you are going through a difficult time, be determined to be free and be healed, God will not refuse anyone who decides to change their lives for the better.

THE MYSTERY OF REDEMPTION AND RECONCILIATION

The work of Christ in the life of the believer is in two phases. We are saved and are being saved. Philippians 2:12-13. The first part of our salvation is that salvation from the wrath of God which restores our relationship with God, the life-giving, eternity bound salvation, and the continual salvation from the works of darkness.

For it PLEASED the FATHER THAT in Him ALL the fullness should dwell, AND by Him to reconcile ALL things to Himself, by Him, whether things on EARTH or things in HEAVEN,

HAVING MADE PEACE through the blood of His cross.
And you, who once were ALIENATED AND enemies
in your mind by wicked works, yet now He HAS reconciled
in the body of His flesh through DEATH, to present you
holy, AND BLAMELESS, AND ABOVE REPROACH in His
sight—if indeed you continue in the FAITH, grounded AND
STEADFAST, AND are not moved AWAY from the hope of the
gospel which you HEARD, which WAS PREACHED to every
CREATURE under HEAVEN, of which I, PAUL, BECAME A
minister.

Colossians 1:19-21

While we are saved and on our way to heaven when we
receive Jesus Christ. We are also being saved continually
from the attacks, and threats of the enemy; the enemy of our
soul as Revelations declares.

Therefore rejoice, O HEAVENS, AND you who dwell in them!
Woe to the INHABITANTS of the EARTH AND the SEA! For
the devil HAS come down to you, HAVING GREAT WRATH,
BECAUSE he knows THAT he HAS A short time."

Revelations 12:12

God knows the wrath of the enemy against all men and most
especially, against those who desire to live godly lives to
please God. He comes after us with great wrath to destroy
our lives and our testimonies but glory be to God who
always leads us in triumph.

But THANKS be to God, who ALWAYS LEADS us in Christ's
TRIUMPHAL procession AND through us SPREADS the
134

AROMA OF the knowledge of Him in every PLACE.

I Corinthians 2:14

God knowing the plans of the enemy, uses the principles of forgiveness to restore us to himself and to restore others who sin against us.

If ANYONE HAS CAUSED PAIN, he HAS CAUSED PAIN not so much to me but to some degree—not to EXAGGERATE—TO ALL of you. This punishment by the MAJORITY is sufficient for THAT person. As A result, you should INSTEAD forgive AND comfort him. Otherwise, he MAY be overwhelmed by excessive grief. Therefore I urge you to REAFFIRM your love to him. I wrote for this purpose: to test your CHARACTER to see if you are obedient in everything. Anyone you forgive, I do too. For WHAT I HAVE forgiven— if I HAVE forgiven ANYTHING—IT is for your benefit in the presence of Christ, so THAT we MAY not be TAKEN ADVANTAGE of by SATAN. For we are not IGNORANT of his schemes.

A Trip to MACEDONIA

When I CAME to TROAS to PREACH the gospel of Christ, even though the Lord opened A door for me, I HAD no rest in my spirit BECAUSE I did not find my brother Titus. INSTEAD, I SAID good-bye to them AND left for MACEDONIA.

A Ministry of Life or DEATH

But THANKS be to God, who ALWAYS LEADS us in Christ's TRIUMPHAL procession AND through us SPREADS the AROMA OF the knowledge of Him in every PLACE.

1 Corinthians 2:5-14

The Lord made me understand that in forgiving those who offended me, I take back the power of the enemy and invite God to rescue and restore my life and to annul what the enemy tried to do in my life. The Lord in my prayer time reminded me of stories of those living, and in the Bible whose life, God redeemed and made better than it ever was.

He reminded me of Ruth and said this to me, it came with such conviction that I knew it was the Lord. He said, Ruth's second husband, did much more for her than her first husband ever did for her.

The Lord gave me specific promises concerning my life. Reaffirmed the things He had told me years ago that I had even forgotten, and I have seen some of the things He told me He would do in my life being manifested.

The core promise that He gave me was that He would do such great work in me that the world can see and can tell a clear distinction between the one who serves and is yielded to God and the one who isn't. I can say God has begun His great work in my life. Opening doors for me, bringing destiny helpers, as I write, I can fell the joy of restoration bubbling up in my spirit and in my heart.

Suddenly my business started to flourish, doors of ministry opened for me and even in the area of relationship I began to see promise.

God is able to take our mess and turn it into a message.

"So I will restore to you the YEARS THAT the SWARMING
[A]LOCUST HAS EATEN,

The CRAWLING locust, The consuming locust, And the
chewing locust,

My GREAT ARMY which I sent AMONG you. You SHALL
EAT in plenty AND be SATISFIED, And PRAISE the NAME of
the Lord your God, Who HAS DEALT wondrously with you;
And My people SHALL never be put to SHAME.

Then you SHALL know THAT I AM in the midst of ISRAEL: I
AM the Lord your God

And there is no other.

My people SHALL never be put to SHAME.

Joel 2:25-27

Key Points:

To achieve wholeness you must be willing to be open and
honest with God. Practice forgiveness through compassion,
worship your way to healing, and get to know the mind of
God and the promises of God for the next chapter and the rest
of your life.

CHAPTER EIGHT

THE SPIRITUAL DIMENSION OF GRIEF

I will no longer talk much with you, for the ruler of this world is coming, and he has nothing in Me.

John 14:30

THE ENTRY WAY

We are fighting an enemy who is deceitful, cunning, and wicked and he waits for every opportunity to strike us. He studies us and devices ways to distract and destroy us. Yet in all of his planning, he will not be successful unless there is an entry given. What is this entryway?

In John 14:30, Jesus alludes to the entryway. The enemy did not have any recourse against the Lord Jesus because there was no sin or guile in Him, nothing that he could work with. The enemy likes to take advantage of our weaknesses and mistakes. He is deceptive, he will play on your weakness and cause you to be confused about the will of God for your life.

The desire of the enemy is to perpetuate an evil occurrence

in the lives of families from generation to generation. Some people do not like to hear and have not taken the time to understand the issue of a generational curse. A generational "curse "does not mean that the person is cursed.

WHAT IS A GENERATIONAL CURSE?

A generational curse is an occurrence of evil perpetuated from generation to generation. Often this curse rides on the will and disobedience of the people involved to transfer it from one generation to the other. If the enemy can succeed in creating a mark of transgression in a family, he works to repeat it in other generations by creating a point of weakness as an entry point.

Therefore, if any man be in Christ, he is a new creature: old things are passed away; behold, all things are become new.
2 Corinthians 5:17

Truly, when we are in Christ, we are born anew and not under any curse. A believer cannot be cursed yet the enemy seeks ways to afflict us through our disobedience and mistakes. In my bloodline, there have been issues of divorce, polygamy, adultery, and relationship instability. Knowing this at an early age, I was bent on breaking the cycle. I fasted many times, prayed, gave a covenant seed offering to ensure that I break the cycle and I believe the Lord heard that and so did the enemy. Yet there remained one thing for me to do, that was my obedience. After I had done all the prayers and given what I had to give, there remained one thing for me to do and that was to say no to the relationships that were not ordained by God. That was something God would not do for me, it had to be an act of my will to say no and that would have exempted me from the pain in my bloodline.

For years, generation after generation, the enemy had afflicted women in my bloodline through the wrong relationships, my mother was a part of that suffering and I was determined to break that cycle yet my disobedience and lack of alignment brought me into the same trap of affliction the enemy had afflicted on the women in my family.

To the young lady who may be reading this book, it is possible for you to escape the pain of your bloodline through your obedience. Obedience is the key that shuts the mouth of hell over your life. Do not think that a one-time disobedience is alright, and you can repent later. The Lord seeks to protect us through our obedience and alignment with His word and His will for our lives, a one-time disobedience is all that the enemy needs to afflict us.

Make a decision and a determination that you will follow and obey the voice of the Lord concerning your life. You have the power to break the cycle.

My son, give attention to my words;
Incline your ear to my sayings.
Do not let them depart from your eyes;
Keep them in the midst of your heart;
For they are life to those who find them,
And health to all their flesh.
Keep your heart with all diligence,
For out of it spring the issues of life.

Proverbs 4:20-27

The Lord wants to protect you, but He needs your obedience and alignment. Your obedience gives way to the Lord for Him to accomplish His purposes in your life without grief. On the contrary, Satan through his cunning deception wants to give you a life of pain grief, and hardship; you decide.

"Now therefore, fear the Lord, serve Him in sincerity and in truth, and put away the gods which your fathers served on the other side of [a]the River and in Egypt. Serve the Lord! 15 And if it seems evil to you to serve the Lord, choose for yourselves this day whom you will serve, whether the gods which your fathers served that were on the other side of [b]the River, or the gods of the Amorites, in whose land you dwell. But as for me and my house, we will serve the Lord."

Joshua 24:14-15

OVERCOMING THE SPIRIT OF GRIEF

Grief is a spirit just as Grace is a Spirit. God gives grace to the humble who adheres to His voice and tremble at is word.

But He gives more grace. Therefore, He says: "God resists the proud, But gives grace to the humble."

James 4:6

God rewards our obedience with His grace and peace. The grace that God gives us is the ability to carry out His purpose and will for our lives and with ease. He blesses us with His peace when we face challenges in our quest to obey and fulfil his purposes. It gives Him joy when we surrender our will to Him and follow His leading.

Therefore the Lord God of Israel says: '... for those who honour Me I will honour, and those who despise Me shall be lightly esteemed.

In that same way, the result of the enemy's attack is grief. Now I need to clarify that grief does not only come as a result of our sins, it comes also as a result of wrongdoing done to us. The intent of the spirit of grief as stated by Jamie Morgan in her article on Charisma, "Spirit of Grief Rises to Take the Fight Out of God's People" was this: 'the enemy sends grief to take the fight out of us and that is exactly how I felt when I was going through my process of mourning'.

The enemy attacks us with the spirit of grief when we experience a loss, death, divorce, and many other situations such as:

- A series of disappointments
- Your heart breaking repeatedly
- The death of a dream from life taking an unexpected direction
- A shattered relationship
- Your heart being battered and bruised from repeated attacks from the enemy
- Anguish over long-term problems
- A myriad of other discouraging, devastating and damaging life events (Charisma, Mag)

The end goal of the enemy is to discourage you from ever pursuing the purposes of God. I remember a dream I had when going through the process of divorce. In the dream I heard two people having a conversation and saying, we will afflict her so badly that she will never forget this experience in her life and will always be sorrowful. But I have good news for you, God's plan is always so much better than the plan of the enemy. He calls us to liberty and freedom.

HOW TO BREAK THE SPIRT OF GRIEF FROM YOUR LIFE

Whenever we are dealing with challenges and difficulties, it is imperative to address it from all angles that is; in the natural and the spiritual and in so doing, we can eradicate that challenge from our lives.

As already discussed, grief is a spirit that enters into our lives through various entryways in our lives. Grief comes to us through the sins we commit or the wrong done to us, or a sheer demonic attack. That is, to shut the door to grief, we must pray as Jazel prayed in 1 Chronicle 4:10.

And Jabez called on the God of Israel saying, "Oh, that You would bless me indeed, and enlarge my [a]territory, that Your hand would be with me, and that You would keep me from evil, that I may not cause pain!" So God granted him what he requested.

Our prayer against the spirit of grief address four things.

- Forgiveness of our sins and disobedience
- Forgiveness for those who the enemy has used to cause us grief
- Wisdom to close the doors we open to the allow the spirit of grief into our lives

- Grace to make the right decisions in our lives
- Deliverance from being victims of other people's sins, mistakes, and weakness
- Freedom from the spirit of spiritual, mental, and emotional oppression

When we make the right decisions that align with the purposes and intents of God for our lives, we close the door to the enemy. Our decision to follow the will of God leads us into safety, therefore closing the doors to the spirit of grief and shame.

Walking in forgiveness brings wholeness, breaks the power of the enemy and keeps him from tormenting you. This is the secret that the Lord taught me and that led me to wholeness. I've been divorced for 2 years but my heart and state of mind is as if I have never been hurt or like I've never experienced the trauma of divorce.

The Lord led me to pray for my ex-husband that he will also find healing and that God will settle him as He is doing in my life. And when I started praying these prayers for him, it was like a flood of cold water being released over my heart and bringing this calmness and healing that has never again relapsed. There is healing in true forgiveness. Grief is a spirit and so is gladness and liberty. Another way to break the spirit of grief is to ask God for the oil of gladness and to activate the liberty of the spirit.

To proclaim the acceptable year of the Lord,
And the day of vengeance of our God;

To comfort all who mourn,
3 To [a]console those who mourn in Zion,
To give them beauty for ashes,
The oil of joy for mourning,
The garment of praise for the spirit of heaviness;
That they may be called trees of righteousness,
The planting of the Lord, that He may be glorified."

Isaiah 61:4

Now the Lord is the Spirit; and where the Spirit of the Lord is,
there is liberty.

2 Corinthians 3:17

MENDING THE BROKEN SPIRIT

The Lord Jesus heals us by mending our broken spirit. Whenever we experience trauma of any kind, there is a part of us that dies. There is a breaking and a death that occurs and this manifests in people in various forms. To have a broken spirit can be understood in two ways, one is to have a humble, gentle, and quiet spirit and that is what the Lord desires of every believer. The second interpretation of a broken spirit is having a bitter soul due to affliction or pain; a state of despair or discouragement.

The manifestation of a broken spirit can be depression, anxiety, feelings of intense hurt, hopelessness, feeling defeated orhaving no hope. Sadly, I experienced most of these feelings going through a divorce.

Dr. Myles Munroe often likened divorce to death, that is; a

146

part of you dies when you go through a divorce. Marriage creates one out of two, therefore a separation from that one brings death to the two. This is the reason why God is the only one who can bring true healing from the trauma of divorce. Many people go through a divorce and ten years later or 20 years later, you find them still hurting and bitter from the divorce. They go through counselling after counselling, therapy after therapy but never find true healing. This is because they seek from man, the kind of healing only God can give. But when you get into the presence of the life giver-Jehovah Rohi, the Shepherd of your soul, He will comfort your soul and breathe new life into you and cause that which is dead to come back to life. How I love Him. The healer of my soul, my bondage breaker, and my heart healer!!

The broken spirit is mended by feeding on the word of God and for those who believe in praying in tongues, it is a sure way to strengthen your inner man. The word of God is like medicine, meditating on it brings healing and with one breath of God at a time, you come to that place of healing. I encourage you right now even before you continue to take some time to pray in the spirit and read Psalm 23. It is possible to be totally and thoroughly healed!!.

When your spirit man is strengthened, you can overcome any challenge that which comes your way. The strength of your inner man determines your ability to overcome the storms of life. Thus, the enemy attacks your spirit man through your emotions and tried to keep you from studying the word, and keeps you from praying. Therefore, it is essential for every believer to strengthen themselves with the study of word and prayer. So long as we live on earth, we will encounter challenges as the enemy will not back away. The wise believer will not wait until they have a challenge before they strengthen themselves in the Lord. Building up yourself in the word of God and prayer, you build a resistance against the enemy so if by any means you fall into his trap through disobedience, the strength of the spirit of God in you is able to strengthen you and cause you to overcome the wilds of the enemy with speed.

A wise believer will rely on their inner strength to recover from the pain of being trapped by the enemy through disobedience, a believer with understanding will rely on their obedience to the word of God, and the promptings of the spirit to escape satanic traps. I was a wise believer, and I relied on my ability to overcome challenges through the tenacious spirit in me developed through the study of the word and prayer. But I discovered a better way to live, that is to live with understanding. I can say I did not have an understanding of the cost of disobedience and the benefits of obedience but now I do.

I made a determination that never again will the enemy gain an advantage over me through disobedience, it will not happen. As long as the Lord lives, and as long as His Spirit directs me, the last victory the enemy had over me will be the very last in my lifetime and in my generations to come.

Keep the word before your eyes, read it even if you feel the Word is not going anywhere. Read it while in tears, read it while in pain, read it while you are happy, and activate it by praying in the spirit and watch your spirit and your life rise like a well-structured edifice.

But ye, beloved, building up yourselves on your most holy faith, praying in the Holy Ghost, Keep yourselves in the love of God, looking for the mercy of our Lord Jesus Christ unto eternal life.

And of some have compassion, making a difference: And others save with fear, pulling them out of the fire; hating even the garment spotted by the flesh. Now unto him that is able to keep you from falling, and to present you faultless before the presence of his glory with exceeding joy

Jude 20-25

And how from childhood you have known the sacred writings (Hebrew Scriptures) which are able to give you the wisdom that leads to salvation through faith which is in Christ Jesus [surrendering your entire self to Him and having absolute confidence in His wisdom, power and goodness].

2 Timothy 3:15

Where you feel like you are falling apart, let your heart rest on the word, it will keep you together. The word of God, believed, and obeyed is our greatest weapon against the wilds of the enemy.

May He grant you out of the riches of His glory, to be strengthened and spiritually energized with power through His Spirit in your inner self, [indwelling your innermost being and personality], so that Christ may dwell in your hearts

through your faith. And may you, having been [deeply] rooted
and [securely] grounded in love.

Ephesians 3:15-17

CHAPTER NINE

THE SUFFERING SERVANT IS OUR COMPASSIONATE HIGH PRIEST

Redemption is God's primary language in this New Testament Era. As a matter of fact, redemption has been God's primary language since the fall of man. Like David, I cannot understand and cannot fully comprehend the love of God towards man. We fail Him yet He is still seeking after us, seeking to restore us. The difference in God's redemption agenda in the old testament and new testament is that, in the old testament, God required man to make continual sacrifices to secure their redemption. In the new testament, Christ has already paid for our sins and redeemed us from the curse of the law, which means even when we miss it, He still remains faithful and waits for our repentance so He can restore us. This was the crease of Jesus's mission.

So He came to Nazareth, where He had been brought up. And as His custom was, He went into the synagogue on the Sabbath day, and stood up to read. And He was handed the book of the prophet Isaiah. And when He had opened the book, He found the place where it was written:

"The Spirit of the LORD is upon Me,
Because He has anointed Me
To preach the gospel to the poor;
He has sent Me [i]to heal the brokenhearted,
To proclaim liberty to the captives
And recovery of sight to the blind,
To set at liberty those who are [j]oppressed;
To proclaim the acceptable year of the LORD."

Luke 4:16-19

Christ has redeemed us from the curse of the law, having become a curse for us (for it is written, "Cursed is everyone who hangs on a tree"), 14 that the blessing of Abraham might come upon the Gentiles in Christ Jesus, that we might receive the promise of the Spirit through faith.

Galatians 3:13-14

Redemption is God foreseeing that man will fail Him and making provision to restore man to Himself. My little children, these things I write to you, so that you may not sin. And if anyone sins, we have an Advocate with the Father, Jesus Christ the righteous. And He Himself is the propitiation for our sins, and not for ours only but also for the whole world.

1 John 2:1-2

Through my experience, I have really come to understand the heart of God for man. God desires not to punish but to restore. When we fail, His primary goal is not to punish us but to heal, deliver, and restore us to the original intent for our lives.

The intent of the enemy in attacking us is to try to stop the purposes of God from manifesting in our lives. God's grand plan of redemption includes you. He wants to reach the world through you and the enemy is trying everything to stop and distract your testimony.

Then Jesus said to them again, "Most assuredly, I say to you, I am the door of the sheep. All who ever came [a]before Me are thieves and robbers, but the sheep did not hear them. I am the door. If anyone enters by Me, he will be saved, and will go in and out and find pasture. The thief does not come except to steal, and to kill, and to destroy. I have come that they may have life, and that they may have it more abundantly.

John 10: 7-10

Your sins, weaknesses, and mistakes are not a surprise to God. God knew every mistake and challenge you would face in your life, yet he still decided to choose you. Your sin, weakness, the iniquity in your bloodline does not intimidate Him. He made an atonement for it before it ever happened. Do not let your missteps, horrific past, and the iniquity at your heel take you away from the will of God. He is in the business of restoring that which is broken.

WHY IS JESUS OUR PERFECT COMFORTER
For every high priest taken from among men is appointed for men in things pertaining to God, that he may offer both gifts and sacrifices for sins. He can [a]have compassion on those who are ignorant and going astray, since he himself is also subject to weakness. 3 Because of this he is required as for the people, so also for himself, to offer sacrifices for sins. And no

man takes this honor to himself, but he who is called by God, just as Aaron was.

A Priest Forever
So also Christ did not glorify Himself to become High Priest, but it was He who said to Him:
"You are My Son,
Today I have begotten You."
As He also says in another place:
"You are a priest forever
According to the order of Melchizedek";
who, in the days of His flesh, when He had offered up prayers and supplications, with vehement cries and tears to Him who was able to save Him from death, and was heard because of His godly fear, 8 though He was a Son, yet He learned obedience by the things which He suffered. And having been perfected, He became the author of eternal salvation to all who obey Him, called by God as High Priest "according to the order of Melchizedek," of whom we have much to say, and hard to explain, since you have become dull of hearing.

The Lord Jesus is our perfect comforter because as Hebrews 5 asserts, He can identify with our weakness and because He Himself has gone through all the challenges that we go through and still came out perfect. And as a perfect lamb of God, He does not look down on us when we fail. The nature of man is such that, when man finds himself having overcome in a certain area of weakness or when a person sees another struggling with something they have control over, there is that tendency to despise those who struggle in that area. But Jesus, in all of His perfections, still sees as

154

His beloved and shows compassion and empathy towards us when we struggle.

To have a deeper understanding of How Christ sees us in our weakness, let that a look at how He handles the woman caught in adultery and Zacchaeus.

THE WOMAN CAUGHT IN ADULTERY

Jesus returned to the Mount of Olives, but early the next morning he was back again at the Temple. A crowd soon gathered, and he sat down and taught them. As he was speaking, the teachers of religious law and the Pharisees brought a woman who had been caught in the act of adultery. They put her in front of the crowd.

"Teacher," they said to Jesus, "this woman was caught in the act of adultery. The law of Moses says to stone her. What do you say?"
They were trying to trap him into saying something they could use against him, but Jesus stooped down and wrote in the dust with his finger. They kept demanding an answer, so he stood up again and said, "All right, but let the one who has never sinned throw the first stone!" Then he stooped down again and wrote in the dust.

When the accusers heard this, they slipped away one by one, beginning with the oldest, until only Jesus was left in the middle of the crowd with the woman. 10 Then Jesus stood up again and said to the woman, "Where are your accusers? Didn't even one of them condemn you?"
"No, Lord," she said.

And Jesus said, "Neither do I. Go and sin no more."

John 8:1-12

CHRIST AND THE ADULTEROUS WOMAN

Christ Jesus operates in the culture of honour, He covers us even in our most vulnerable state, even when we are wrong. Human nature seeks to shame and expose but when we learn to forgive and cover the weaknesses of others, we save relationships and sometimes even the very lives of people. Sometimes we need to draw the line between speaking truth to a situation and covering the nakedness of others while still bringing truth to light. Truth must be spoken in love and in a manner that covers the shame of others.

Christ protected and defended the adulterous woman from her accusers with one question.

The woman was already feeling ashamed by her sins and her accusers. Instead of chastening and humiliating her, Christ protected her honour by not joining her accusers in condemning her. That is exactly what He does for us when our sins and that of others bring us to a point of shame and reproach. He is the lifter of our heads. When you are feeling shamed and abused, remember He is your Glory and the one who lifts your head.

Many are they who say of me, "There is no help for him in God." Selah. But You, O Lord, are a shield [a]for me, My glory and the One who lifts my head.

Psalm 3:2-3

LESSON FROM THE ADULTEROUS WOMAN'S ENCOUNTER WITH JESUS

- Jesus gave her His approval and acceptance. Not an approval and acceptance of her sin but an approval that despite her sins and iniquities, she is still loved and accepted. God loves the sinner and hates the sin.
- Jesus called her into a new life, "Go and Sin No More". This statement was a calling into a deeper and sanctified life. Later we see this woman, returning to Jesus and pouring out her Alabaster box of oil in love before the one who rescued her.

God is not interested in punishing us in this dispensation of Grace. Yes, we may face the natural consequences of our sins but He is there to heal, restore, and make whole.

JESUS IS FOR THE WEAK AND BROKEN AND ALSO FOR THE RICH AND POWERFUL

The Story of Zacchaeus, The Tax Collector

Jesus entered Jericho and was passing through. A man was there by the name of Zacchaeus; he was a chief tax collector and was wealthy. He wanted to see who Jesus was, but because he was short he could not see over the crowd. So he ran ahead and climbed a sycamore-fig tree to see him, since Jesus was coming that way.

When Jesus reached the spot, he looked up and said to him, "Zacchaeus, come down immediately. I must stay at your house today." So he came down at once and welcomed him gladly.

All the people saw this and began to mutter, "He has gone to be the guest of a sinner." But Zacchaeus stood up and said to the Lord, "Look, Lord! Here and now I give half of my possessions to the poor, and if I have cheated anybody out of anything, I will pay back four times the amount."

Jesus said to him, "Today salvation has come to this house, because this man, too, is a son of Abraham. 10 For the Son of Man came to seek and to save the lost."

LESSON FROM THE STORY OF ZACCHAEUS

- God does not discriminate. He is the God of the rich and the God of the poor. Often, we are quick to discrete the pain and needs of the rich and powerful. We presuppose that because they have economic stability and power, we think they have no other needs and do not experience brokenness just like any other person. The beauty of God is that He knows exactly what the heart needs.

- Jesus has time for you and willing to give you the attention you need. Zaccheus encountered Jesus when he was on His way to Jerusalem. In the natural, it seemed that Zacchaeus was not scheduled into Jesus's itinerary. Yet Jesus was kind enough to interrupt his own plans and make plans for Zacchaeus.

- He is the God who will leave the 99 and attend to the one person who is broken and needs comfort and companionship. What is your need today? Do you need forgiveness, compassion, companionship? Call on Jesus, He will answer and will not leave you alone.

- Jesus is not afraid to be seen with the outcast. The sins of the outcast do not intimidate the Lord Jesus. He puts his reputation on the line to associate with the outcast.

Are you feeling like an outcast? Call on the lover of outcasts and He will be your companion.

CHAPTER TEN

GOD'S SYSTEM OF COMPENSATION & RESTORATION

G od is in the business of restoring and compensating us for the loss and pain we have experienced.

'He will wipe every tear from their eyes. There will be no more death'[a] or mourning or crying or pain, for the old order of things has passed away."

Rev. 21:4

There is a promise of restoration and compensation at the return of the Lord Jesus. Yet while on earth, He has a process of restoration and compensation for us.

"I will repay you for the years the locusts have eaten—
  the great locust and the young locust,
  the other locusts and the locust swarm[b]—
my great army that I sent among you.
You will have plenty to eat, until you are full,
  and you will praise the name of the Lord your God,
  who has worked wonders for you;
never again will my people be shamed.

Then you will know that I am in Israel,
that I am the Lord your God,
and that there is no other;
never again will my people be shamed. Joel 2:26-27

God's system of restoration is in three parts.
- Forgiveness of sins (Mercy)
- Restoration of lost time, years, and resources
- Restoration of your reputation (Social and Spiritual)

MERCY

It is the compassion of God that moves Him to have mercy on us. Without mercy, there is no room for repentance and restoration. We are saved because God is merciful.

In the book of Lamentations, the Prophet Jeremiah records his famous text on the mercies of God.

Through the Lord's mercies we are not consumed,
Because His compassions fail not. 23 They are new every morning;
Great is Your faithfulness.

Lamentations 3:22-23

The mercies of God allow God to forgive us of our sins. Some define mercy as God forgiving us our sins and not giving us the punishment, we deserve. Once the mercy and forgiveness of God sets in, He then extends to our compassion, which is also translated as grace. Throughout the gospels, whenever Jesus was about to perform a miracle, the gospels record, and "He had compassion".

The compassion of Jesus is what leads Him to restore to us what we have lost. He can sympathize with our pain, loss, and frustration and when He feels the pains of our heart, He is moved to comfort us and provide solutions for us. There is the grace that restores what we have lost and the grace that is able to keep that which God has restored to us.

THE THREEFOLD RESTORATION
Beloved, I pray that you may prosper in all things and be in health, just as your soul prospers.

3 John 2

The tripartite nature of man is such that if one part of the body suffers, there is a potential that the other parts of the body will suffer. Therefore, when a time of visitation comes, God seeks to restore the person entirely. That is, a person who has been afflicted in their health is most likely afflicted in their finance, emotional and mental health.

I can gladly say the Lord has prospered my business and completely restored me emotionally. I have experienced financial prosperity much more than any other year in my entire life and it is only going to get better and better. Thus, when the visitation of the Lord comes, He restores all areas of our lives so we can be whole.

In the above scripture, the Apostle John talks about prospering in health, soul, and in finance.

HOW CAN WE RECEIVE SUCH RESTORATION?
Restoration begins when we recognize our need for God.

When we recognize our need for him, whether we have caused harm or harm has been done to us, His ears are open and attentive to our cry.

Therefore the Lord will wait, that He may be gracious to you; And therefore He will be exalted, that He may have mercy on you. For the Lord is a God of justice; Blessed are all those who wait for Him.

Often I see people who have suffered loss and grief because of a wrong that's been done to them and instead of crying out to God and calling to him for mercy and compensation, the result is taking matters into their own hands.

They become vengeful, angry, bitter, and sometimes rebellious, turning away from God. When you are wronged, God sees it and He waits to show mercy and rectify the situation but if we disregard the due process of God and take matters into our own hands, we stifle the hand of God from moving on our behalf.

As a father, God has the best vengeance and restoration is complete. It is one that is able to bring reconciliation and healing the restore or replace whatever we have lost. Yet we forget vengeance is His and that He will do a better job at it than we could ever ask for.

Coming to God for solution means humbling ourselves to receive His mercy. That is, there must be an acknowledgement of our sins and iniquity. When we lay down our sins, we can then take on his strength, mercy, and compensation.

It also requires that we lay down any unforgiveness for the restoration that God has in store for us.

I trust in the pages of this book, you have come to see the Lord as He is, the God of all comfort.

DO NOT FORFEIT RESTORATION

One of the worst things that could happen in a person's life is for them to forfeit their blessings and compensations. God is a God of systems and principles and as much as He loves and desires to show us His mercies and goodness, He wants us to adhere and respond to the principles He has put in place for us to access His grace.

Some of such principles is that we must forgive and not take vengeance of our own. There was a gentleman who was abandoned by his father when he was a baby and reconnected with him at age 16. His siblings were unkind and really mistreated him. The truth is, the father loved this son of his and he bore many resemblances to him. This young man was very kind-hearted and had the spirit of servitude. After two years of living with his father and his stepsiblings, he broke and rebelled due to mistreatment from his stepmom and stepsiblings. From then on He went on a mission to give his father real grief.

This sweet young man changed and became rebellious and antagonistic towards his father and did everything to sabotage his father who occupied a very prominent position. This went on for years and to the extent that his father grew very bitter and angry towards this young man and took him out of his Will.

The father's desire was to make up for the years he lost with this child by giving him a greater portion of his properties at his inheritance. Yet, when the Will and Testament of the father were read, the son broke down in tears because all the father left for him was his wishes rather than intended properties he had in store.

You see, the father wanted to compensate the child for the pain and suffering he went through as a child by giving him a greater portion of his inheritance but this child through bitterness, anger, and rebellion, threw away the blessings that was due to come to him.

May you never be at a place when you are too grieved to be comforted. The Lord is close to the broken heart and saves those who are willing and open-hearted.

he Lord is close to the brokenhearted
and saves those who are crushed in spirit.
The righteous person may have many troubles,
but the Lord delivers him from them all;

Psalm 34:18-19

The surest way to have the almighty God on your side is the accept his gift of salvation. The Bible says for all have sinned and fallen short of the glory of God. Yet he makes room for us and opens the door for repentance.

If you have read this book till the end and you don't know

the Lord Jesus as your saviour.

But what does it say? "The word is near you, in your mouth and in your heart" (that is, the word of faith which we preach): that if you confess with your mouth the Lord Jesus and believe in your heart that God has raised Him from the dead, you will be saved. For with the heart one believes unto righteousness, and with the mouth confession is made unto salvation

If you do wish to accept the Lord Jesus as your saviour and Lord, please say this prayer after me.

Dear Lord Jesus, thank you for loving me and fighting for me even when I didn't know you. Today I accept you as my Saviour and Lord. I will live for you, I will obey you, and I will allow your love to flow through me. Father, I surrender my life to you. Please take all of me, heal me, deliver me, and let your will be done in my life. Holy Spirit, please come into my life and be my guide, this I pray in Jesus name.

Now if you have accepted the Lord as your saviour, Ask the Lord to lead you to a Bible believing church. Purchase a Bible and look for other Christian resources online to assist you in your journey of faith.

Welcome home. I will be glad to hear about your decision to follow the Lord Jesus. You can email me at ***principlesht@ gmail.com.***

The Lord bless you and may the healing river of God flow over your heart. Shalom

SOURCES

New King James Version
New International Version
https://www.betterhealth.vic.gov.au/health/healthyliving/
anger-how-it-affects-people

ABOUT THE BOOK

The God of All Comfort is about experiencing the healing and the comfort of God through various seasons and forms of grief. In this book, we explore the stories of Bible Characters who experienced tremendous grief yet overcame their pain with the help of God.

I share with you my personal experiences of grief, growing up in a broken home to making bad decisions, and disobedience to the Holy Spirit that led to seasons of failure and pain. As a recent divorcee, I share with you my experience of going through the horrible pit of pain and rejection and how I found grace and healing in the presence of God.

I have experienced the love of God in such a tremendous way that my heart feels as though It had never been hurt. The God of all comfort does indeed comfort and heal.

My prayer is that through these pages, the rejected, broken, divorced, and the one who feels responsible for their pain will find healing in Christ and be filled with a love that is not humanly possible to attain but truly divine, that is, the divine love of God.

God turned my ashes into treasures by showing me mercy and Love. May He do the same for you as you turn the pages of this book. Shalom!!

ABOUT THE AUTHOR

Priscilla Serwaa -Boateng is a young lady who loves the Lord and serves His purposes. She is the Founder and Owner of Vessels Recruitment Services. She is a Singer, Songwriter, a Bible Teacher and the Host of Principles and Hidden Treasures, The Restored Woman, and Principled Kids &Teens. These teaching programs are dedicated to teaching the principles of God, and building young people for a Christ-Centred victorious living. The Restored Woman is a teaching program dedicated to marriages, relationships, and finding wholeness in Christ.

Priscilla's greatest passion is for intimacy with the Holy Spirit, the study of the work, prayer, and to see the broken healed and restored to God.

She is a member of the Church of Pentecost, Canada, and enjoys drawing the heart of people to God through music, teaching of the word, and prayer. You can follow her on:
- The Restored Woman and Principles and Hidden Treasure
- @therestored_woman and @principlesandhidd
- and our children's page @ Principled_kids_teens
- Principles and Hidden Treasure
- Principled_Kids_Teens

Printed in Great Britain
by Amazon